A VIEW *from the* CLIFFS

THE EAST DEVON HERITAGE COAST

Edited by Richard Butler

DEVON BOOKS

First published 1986 by Devon Books
Copyright © Devon County Council, 1986
ISBN 0-86114-761-8

British Library Cataloguing in Publication Data

East Devon Heritage Coast
   1. East Devon Heritage Coast (England)
   I. Butler, Richard K.
   914.23'57   SB484.G7

This book has been produced on behalf of the Amenities and Countryside
Committee of Devon County Council. It was compiled and edited by R. K.
Butler, the Heritage Coast Officer in the Amenities and Countryside Division
of the County Property Department. The Director of Property is Andrew Smy
and the Amenities and Countryside Officer is Peter Hunt.

DEVON BOOKS

Publishers to the Devon County Council

Devon Books is a division of A. Wheaton & Co. Ltd who represents:

Design, Editorial & Publicity
Production & Manufacturing
A. Wheaton & Co. Ltd, Hennock Road, Exeter EX2 8RP
Tel: 0392-74121   Telex: 42749 (WHEATN G)
(A. Wheaton & Co. Ltd is a division of Pergamon Press)

Sales & Distribution
Town & Country Books, 24 Priory Avenue, Kingskerswell,
Newton Abbot TQ12 5AQ   Tel: 08047-2690

CONTENTS

From red marl to chalk: cliffs between Sidmouth and Beer

Otter estuary (left)

ACKNOWLEDGEMENTS

The editor and publishers wish to thank the following for providing the illustrations reproduced in this book.

Beer Parish Council: p. 65
Barbara Benfield: pp. 11, 12, 13, 14, 15
Henneke Coates: pp. 62, 63
Devon Archaeological Society and the British Museum: p. 30 (right)
R. Harriss: pp. 9, 34 (left), 43, 44, 45, 46, 47
David Nichols: pp. 21, 22, 23, 32
Margaret Parkinson: p. 25
Revd H. Rann: p. 34 (right)
Royal Albert Memorial Museum, Exeter: p. 30 (left)
Peter Thomas: pp. 16, 17, 18, 19, 20
Other photographs are by Devon County Council.

The geological cross-section on p. 6 is reproduced by permission of the Director, British Geological Survey (NERC): Crown/NERC copyright reserved.

Maps are reproduced from the Ordnance Survey 1:50 000 maps with the permission of the Controller of Her Majesty's Stationery Office, Crown copyright reserved.

Cover: *Looking east from Ladram Bay to High Peak and Sidmouth*

Title page: *View west across Weston Mouth to Rempstone Rocks*

INTRODUCTION

Lying between the Exe estuary to the west and Lyme Regis to the east, the coastline of east Devon contains a rich variety of landscapes which represent one of the most outstanding and diversified coastal areas in England and Wales.

The contrasts are endless. Rich agricultural land, woodland and heath, deep and sheltered combes, wide flat estuaries, thriving tourist resorts, quiet hamlets, traditional rural skills, modern agricultural practices—and all within a natural landscape that is ever changing to captivate and stretch the imagination.

It was in recognition of these qualities, so long loved and appreciated by its local inhabitants, that the area was designated as a Heritage Coast by the Countryside Commission in 1984. Only forty such stretches of coastline exist in England and Wales, and it is hoped that, within each, measures will be introduced to control development rigorously and to look after the environment so that people can live, work and enjoy the area in harmony.

This will not be an easy task. Our coastal areas have long catered for the demands of agriculture, industry, housing and recreation. This will continue and may increase to an extent where further irreparable damage will occur within what is part of our national heritage. It may be the destruction of a wildlife habitat, the disappearance of an ancient right of way, or the loss of a view enjoyed by countless generations.

Much can be achieved through encouragement and persuasion, through advice and small-scale financial incentives, or through better levels of information and by working together. This is the very essence of Heritage Coast management as now practised within this coastal area.

It is hoped that this book can play a part in achieving those goals by highlighting, through the eyes of local people with varying specialist knowledge, the different aspects of this coast which make it worthy of its place as one of the most outstanding coastlines of our nation. If it can do this, then its purpose will have been served.

Each chapter is based on one of a series of leaflets produced by Devon County Council as part of its Heritage Coast Service. Some have been extended to include that stretch of the east Devon coastline between Exmouth and Budleigh Salterton which lies outside the Heritage Coast.

The Ordnance Survey map extracts on the following three pages are taken from the O.S. Sheets 192 and 193 in the 1:50 000 series. They show the east Devon coastline which extends for 25 miles from the Exe estuary to the Dorset border.

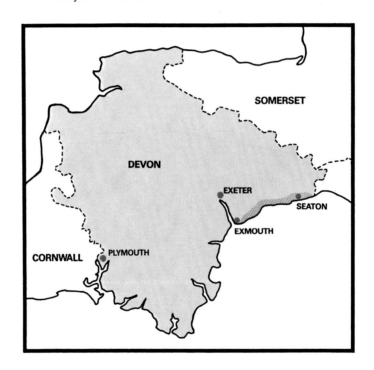

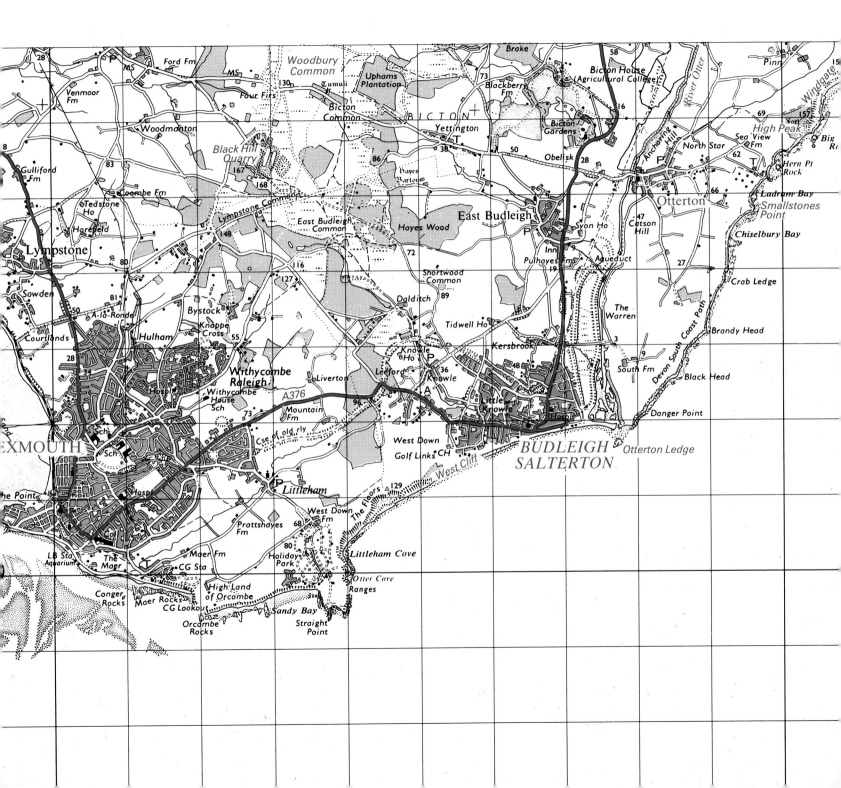

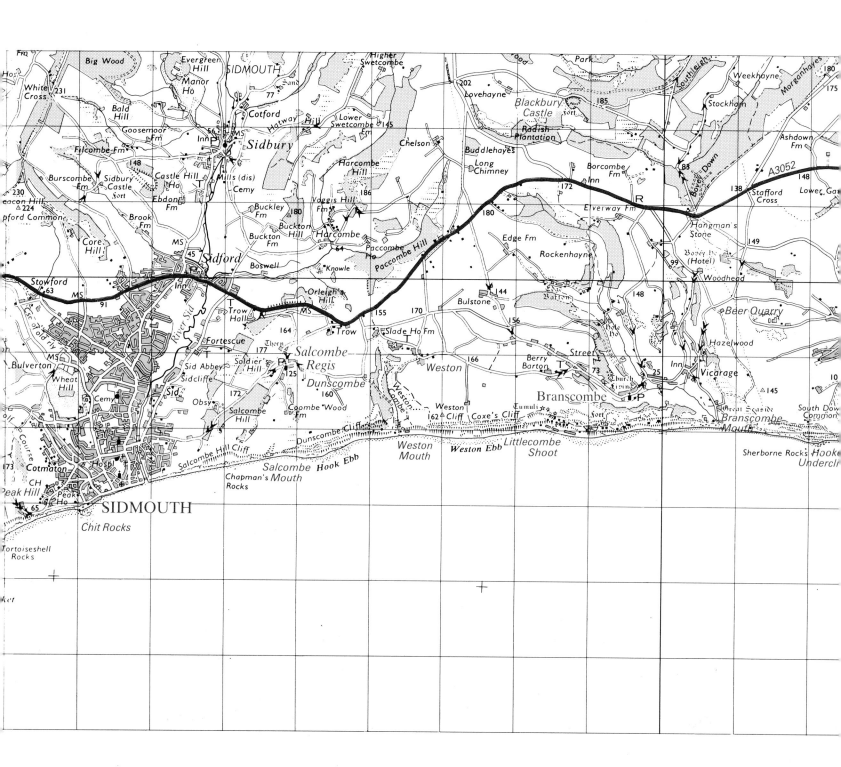

View west from Hooken Undercliffs

Clay with flints overlying the chalk at Dunscombe Cliffs

1 SETTING *the* SCENE

The interrelationship of man's activity with the controlling influences of nature have produced, over millions of years, the many and varied landscapes that we see all around us today. The landscapes of east Devon are no exception to this rule, but, whereas the excesses of man's activity in some places may have been responsible for the degradation of those areas, a balance seems to have been reached here.

This theme of interrelationship between man and nature is inescapable and one that is repeated through the chapters of this book. Nature influences the shape of the land and its climate; these in turn influence settlement patterns, the use to which the land is put and the overall appearance of the landscape.

It is only in more recent years that the technological advances that have been made, in the sphere of agriculture and in the exploration for, and processing of, oil and gas, appear to threaten this balance nationally, and we need to be very aware of the consequences that this could have for our rural and coastal environments.

The east Devon coastline extends for some twenty-five miles from the Exe estuary in the west to the Dorset border. It lies at the end of the motorway network into the south-west peninsula and is easily accessible to the people of the Midlands conurbation as well as London and the south-east. About 56 000 people live within the area, just over half in the town of Exmouth. Most of the remainder live in the resorts of Sidmouth, Seaton and Budleigh Salterton, with small numbers living in the villages, hamlets and farms dotted through the coastal belt. In recent years population growth has been fairly stable, although large numbers of retired people are attracted to the area by its mild climate and pleasant environment.

The scenic attractions of the area are well documented. Deep valleys separated by high plateaux, steep cliff faces and headlands towering above pebble or sandy beaches and changing from red sandstone in the west to chalk and softer shales in the east, produce a variety and charm distinctively different from the rest of Devon.

The juxtaposition of the different rock types, their inherent instability and the constant changes of slope hold an equal fascination for both the geologist and the naturalist, and a visit to the more dramatic areas, such as the Hooken Undercliff or Dowlands Landslip, with their broken and untamed terrain, cannot but enthral.

Most of the area is farmed. In the west, large arable fields near the coast, which have witnessed the gradual removal of hedgerows, give way inland to a patchwork of smaller fields used for grazing. The land rises steeply from the valley of the Otter to the moorlands and commons to the north-west and the conifer woodland above Sidmouth. East of Sidmouth the high flat tableland is a mix of grassland and arable, cut by deep combes with bracken-covered or wooded upper slopes and rich alluvial bottoms. East of the Axe estuary the land again rises steeply. The cliffs and valley slopes are often tree-covered, with extensive fields of arable and grazing land inland.

Looking east along the coast from Beer Head

Table 1 Areas of importance for nature conservation

Name	Location	Comment
National Nature Reserve		
Axmouth–Lyme Regis Undercliffs	Between Seaton and Lyme Regis	793 acres (321 ha) of international importance as a coastal site; geological, woodland, remote wildlife community importance.
Sites of Special Scientific Interest		
Exe Estuary	Exmouth	International ornithological importance, particularly for waders and wildfowl. Geological interest at Orcombe Point.
Budleigh Salterton Cliffs	Budleigh Salterton	A fine section of Bunter Pebble Beds and adjacent deposits; proposed boundary changes will make this site 26 acres (10.6 ha).
Windgate Cliffs	Sidmouth	Fine coastal cliffs exposing the most westerly extension of chalk in England; 114 acres (46 ha).
Salcombe Regis to Beer Coast	Between Salcombe Mouth and Beer	Geological interest; chalk grassland with interesting plants and insects; 812 acres (328.6 ha).
Beer Stone Quarry	Beer	Beer stone outcrop of stratigraphical importance; 141 acres (57.2 ha).
Ware Cliffs	Lyme Regis	Part of Axmouth–Lyme Regis landslip; 41 acres (16.6 ha).
Devon Trust for Nature Conservation Reserves		
Sidmouth Cliffs Nature Reserve	Sidmouth	Mostly cliff face; nature trail; 18.6 acres (7.4 ha).
Weston Mouth Nature Reserve	Weston	Interesting wildlife and plant habitat; rarities recorded; 3.5 acres (1.4 ha).
Otter Estuary Nature Reserve	Budleigh Salterton	Intertidal salt-marshes of botanical and ornithological interest; 45 acres (18.2 ha).
Other reserves		
Axe Estuary Borrowpit Lagoon Nature Reserve	Axe estuary	Valuable refuge for wildlife and as a resting, breeding and feeding place for birds.
Sites listed as being of especial value for birds		
Otter Estuary and Salt-marsh	Budleigh Salterton	
Otterton Ledge–Smallstones Point	Between Budleigh Salterton and Ladram Bay	
East Budleigh Common	East Budleigh	
Mutters Moor	Sidmouth	
Boshill Wood	Axmouth	
Axe Estuary	Seaton	
Axmouth–Lyme Regis Undercliffs	Between Seaton and Lyme Regis	
Woodland Trust Sites		
Page Wood	Sidmouth	Deciduous woodland; 1.3 acres (0.5 ha).

The importance of this stretch of coast for nature conservation is emphasized by the seemingly endless number of statutory designations. Two-thirds of the coastline have some form of protection, and it is particularly interesting for its geological variety, its wildlife communities, its lime-loving plants and the general diversity of habitats. Among the special areas are the National Nature Reserve between Axmouth and Lyme Regis, the internationally recognized Exe estuary, nearly 1000 acres of Sites of Special Scientific Interest and the local nature reserves on the Otter and the Axe and the area east of Sidmouth.

The edge of the sea is also of great interest and value for nature conservation, especially the areas of Smallstones Point, off Ladram Bay, and off Beer Head.

The long history of settlement in the area is reflected in the large number of archaeological sites dating back thousands of years to prehistoric times. The most obvious are the numerous round mounds (barrows) on nearby Woodbury Common or at Farway on the edge of the area. Evidence of prehistoric settlement has been recorded at Beer Head, Salcombe Hill and on Mutter's Moor, where many thousands of worked flints have been found. At Hawkesdown Hill near Axmouth and at Berry Cliff near Branscombe are defensive earthwork sites known as hill-forts.

The Romans were also prominent in the area, evidenced by the well-known villa site at Seaton, and, following the Roman withdrawal in A.D. 410, a Celtic trading-post was established at High Peak, Otterton. By the time of the Domesday survey all the village sites and several of the farm sites in the area had been settled.

Links between the towns, villages and countryside remained central to their prosperity well into the twentieth century. More recently, ties have been loosened, as tourism and the popularity of this area for retirement play increasing roles in the local economy. Inevitably, this has led to changes in the character of the towns and villages, and places like Beer, once a fishing village, are now popular resorts, catering for thousands of visitors each year.

The sense of history is evoked by the many fine old buildings, which have survived the changes through the centuries and may be found in imposing terraces in the town or in splendid isolation in a more rural setting. Exmouth, a resort for more than 200 years, reflects the prosperity of those Georgian and late-Victorian days in much of its architecture, while Sidmouth similarly prospered in Regency times, when the Napoleonic wars curtailed travel abroad. Today's settlement pattern is dominated by the resorts, but escape to those quiet hamlets and byways, where one can still be forgiven for believing that time has stood still, is never far away.

The economy of the area is very strongly based on agriculture and tourism and their associated services, and on local commerce. Small industrial estates on the edge of some of the larger towns provide further diversification, while fewer numbers are now employed in fishing, forestry and quarrying. The way in which the land is farmed affects not only the appearance of the landscape but also the opportunities for employment. The land is rich – among the

View eastwards from Salcombe Hill

The Otter estuary

Sidmouth from the west

most fertile in Britain – with dairy farming and cereal growing predominating, while sheep- and cattle-rearing account for most of the other farming activity. With the advent of mechanization, farming has become much more productive, but the numbers of people directly employed on the land has fallen significantly.

The effect of quarrying or mining on the area is very localized. Whereas once the calcareous marls were dug from many local pits for agricultural use and flints were picked from the fields and used for building, activities are now restricted to the Beer quarries, where lime is abstracted, and to Dunscombe, where stone is quarried for repair works to Exeter Cathedral.

Woodland is not extensive in the area and is confined to land

unsuitable for agriculture, such as steep slopes, exposed higher ground and the more poorly drained soils. Small plantations of conifer woodland are to be found on the east Devon commons, around Sidmouth and on either side of the Axe estuary. Other informal woodlands, consisting of deciduous and indigenous trees, contribute to the landscape through their variety of form, seasonal changes of colour and their wildlife value, but they have not been exploited commercially.

Commercial fishing takes place on a small scale from Seaton, Sidmouth and Beer, and more significantly from Exmouth. The fishermen often supplement their income during the holiday season by combining their normal activities with taking tourists on fishing trips. The main catch is shellfish, which are caught between March and September, and mainly sold outside the area; some bass, skate, plaice and mackerel are also landed and sold locally.

It is the tourist industry that has rapidly become one of the mainstays of the local economy in east Devon. Each year about 440 000 visitors come to the area and spend £46 million (see Table 2). The traditional forms of holiday accommodation, the hotels and guest houses, no longer cater for the majority of staying visitors. Only 19 per cent now stay in such accommodation, the vast majority preferring the freedom and lower costs of self-catering chalets, caravans and tents. These are to be found on a variety of large and small sites scattered along the coastal belt, but, as Table 3 shows, it is still the resort areas of Exmouth, Seaton and Sidmouth that provide the greatest range of accommodation.

The benefits of tourism to the area are undeniable, but it should also be remembered that at the peak of the season considerable disruption to local communities occurs. This may take several different forms: noise, litter, disturbance, traffic or simply sheer numbers of people. To satisfy the demands of both the visitor and the resident will often require great tact and patience, and sometimes may not be possible.

The scene is now set for a trip into and along the East Devon Heritage Coast, to unravel its mysteries and enjoy its unfolding panoramas, through the eyes of local people who live and work there or visit it frequently. It may not be enough simply to read about this enchanting coastline; you will most probably wish to visit it and explore at first hand. Opportunities abound! Although most of the area is privately owned, there is a dense network of public rights of way allowing access on foot to most parts. The South Devon

Caravan site near Beer Head

Coast Path winds its way through the whole length of the coastline, and numerous paths lead from it alongside the estuaries or into open countryside. Woodland and common tracks provide other opportunities for walking and riding, while, for the less energetic, a trip by car along country lanes may be the order of the day. Please remember, however, whenever you are walking, driving or riding in the countryside or its villages, to respect its life and work and to follow the Country Code.

Table 2   Total number of tourist nights in east Devon, 1984*

Hotels and guest houses	Flats and cottages	Chalets	Static caravans	Touring caravans	Tents	Private houses	Total
849 500	230 000	419 500	1 235 000	384 000	185 000	1 067 000	4 370 000

Table 3   Capacity (bedspaces) of holiday accommodation in resorts, 1984*

	Hotels and guest houses	Flats and cottages	Chalets	Static caravans	Touring caravans	Tents	Total
Exmouth	1 600	720	610	6 210	720	400	10 260
Seaton	440	330	2 260	310	460	540	4 340
Sidmouth	2 230	320	–	280	160	240	3 230
Rest of east Devon	1 960	930	480	4 610	4 610	2 080	14 670

* Source: Devon Tourism Review 1984, Devon County Council

2 | ROCKS *and* FOSSILS

The structural movements and weathering processes that have taken place on the rock strata of the Heritage Coast have led to the creation of a landscape unlike any that occurs elsewhere in Devon. Plunging valleys emerge at the coast alongside high, flat tableland areas, with spectacular cliff faces and headlands rising above pebbly beaches between Budleigh Salterton and Lyme Regis. At certain sections along the cliff there have been landslips of the strata, which give an added interest to the observer.

The deposition of the rocks that underlie the present landscape has taken place over a period of more than 200 million years and the processes of erosion by wind, rain and sea are continuing. Examination of the layers of rock exposed in the cliff faces provides evidence of the sequence in which these rocks were laid down and subsequently deformed by massive earth movements. The characteristics of the sandstones, sand and gravels, chalk and mudstones, together with shells of marine creatures, indicate that these deposits were laid down in a shallow sea.

A clear sequence of rocks can be seen from the red sandstones and marls between the Otter estuary and Sidmouth, to the yellow-coloured Greensand cliffs capped with flints and gravels around Salcombe and Weston Mouth, to the chalk cliffs of Beer and the softer shales east of Seaton. Changing outcrops give rise to changes in slope and vegetation. The Greensand generally produces steeply sloping land, often covered by rough grass and gorse, while the adjacent marls lower down the valleys lead to gentler slopes with better soils.

The relationship between the strata is best observed from offshore, though by following the coast path, an excellent appreciation of the sequence of deposition of rocks (stratigraphy) and the inherent fauna of these ancient times (palaeontology), as well as of the visual beauty of the landscape, can be gleaned.

Geological cross-section of the east Devon coastline

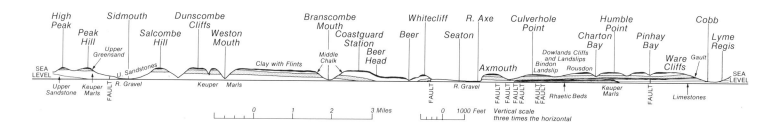

6

Geological history

The outcrops of rock visible along the east Devon coast are relatively young in geological terms, having been deposited within the last 230 million years (Ma). The county as a whole was largely 'formed' by the end of the Triassic (195 Ma). It is likely that Cretaceous, Jurassic and maybe Triassic strata, which are now present only in east Devon, once covered most of the county. However, subsequent erosion has revealed a land surface of former times, which has been modified from its original mountainous desert to produce a land-form of scenic and geological diversity.

Following the formation of the Dartmoor Granite about 280 Ma, there was an uplift, which caused mountains that must have been 10 000 feet high, with associated deep valleys. The climate at the time was arid with infrequent violent rain storms which caused large amounts of sediment to be swept down into the valleys and desert plains. Weathering of this material turned all iron compounds into red oxides and hence the red colouration of the New Red Sandstones of the Permian. The scenery of Devon some 250 Ma must have been similar at that time to the southern fringes of the Sahara Desert today, although with much fewer flora and fauna.

The sands with coarse pebbles, which can be seen in the cliffs between Budleigh Salterton and the mouth of the River Otter, were laid down from 230 Ma, in the bed of a great river. The source of the pebbles now appears to be western France, the inference being that the English Channel at that time was then a single desert basin across which a large river could flow.

At about 195 Ma there was a marine advancement, which laid down the White Lias (as seen at Pinhay Bay), followed by the long shelf sea deposition of the Jurassic. Most of Devon continued as a land mass except for a trough extending across central Devon north of Exeter to Crediton and Hatherleigh.

At the beginning of the Cretaceous (about 105 Ma) there was a marked marine advancement. The Upper Greensand (as seen at Beer) was deposited in a shallow sea, which extended to cover large areas of the county but which probably left Dartmoor and Exmoor as islands. During this period there were minor phases of folding and faulting, which affected the strata of east Devon immediately before the deposition of the Upper Greensand, producing an easterly dip. Some deformations are evident which affected the Upper Greensand around Beer before the chalk was deposited, giving rise to a series of small-scale domes and basins.

The sea finally retreated from Devon in the late Cretaceous or early Tertiary, but the geological evolution continued. Uplift of the land area at about 50 Ma under a sub-tropical climate led to deep weathering and erosion of the chalk elsewhere in the county. The chalk outcrop in east Devon is the westernmost occurrence in the country.

The Alpine Orogeny (a period of mountain building about 20 Ma) had little effect on Devon as a whole, although some minor faulting and warping is evident in the chalk at Beer.

The county achieved its final form by the end of the Pliocene (2 Ma), though almost certainly the land extended well beyond the present coastline, and subsequent erosion has led to the existing line of cliffs.

Geological processes are still continuing, but in a human life-span it is not always possible to appreciate such change. Certain events, however, such as storms, floods and landslips can bring about sudden and dramatic changes to topography, both coastal and inland.

Recent history and existing land-form

The following is a description of the rock outcrops together with the recent history of mineral workings between Budleigh Salterton and Lyme Regis.

The coarse red gravel and sand deposits of the Budleigh Salterton Pebble Beds occur in a sequence of about 80 feet thick to the west of the town. The strata exhibit cross bedding which gives an indication of former river currents, the material having been laid down by a river flowing northwards from France. Inland, the Pebble Beds form an escarpment with an easterly dip slope and supporting a barren heathland in the form of the east Devon commons. These sand and gravel deposits are extensively quarried on Woodbury Common at Blackhill Quarry and provide a significant resource of construction aggregates, exending in a narrow belt northwards to Somerset, the Midlands and the north-east of England.

Eastwards, between the mouth of the River Otter and Sidmouth, a sequence of coarse red sandstones with some pebbles can be seen which overlie the Pebble Beds.

The red cliffs rising to about 160 feet and framing Sidmouth are the Keuper Marls. They are composed of thin sandstones at the base, with bands of gypsum and rock-salt in the thickly bedded mudstones above. The marls give rise to higher quality agricultural land in the valleys inland. The bands of gypsum were worked many years ago on a small scale just west of Littlecombe Shoot between Sidmouth and Branscombe. The Marls were dug extensively in the area, and especially in the Sid valley prior to the nineteenth century, to be used as a top dressing on farmland.

To the east of Sidmouth there is a marked colour change in the cliff faces to a sandy yellow as the Upper Greensand of the Cretaceous period becomes evident. The plateau rises to about 550 feet at this point, and on the coast it is characterized by steep cliffs with flints and gravel capping the yellow Greensand and the white chalk. The plateau is dissected by deep valleys at the 'mouths' of Salcombe, Weston and Branscombe, which have been cut into the underlying marls and sandstones. A distinctive change in slope and vegetation is evident, as the steeply sloping Greensands of the valley sides merge into the gentler slopes of the softer marls in the valley bottoms.

The cliffs gradually fall to the east, and the beds are best exposed at Whitecliff, near Seaton, where the Cretaceous strata are faulted against Keuper Marl. Here can be seen some 80 feet of greenish grey sands with overlying Chert Beds of about 65 feet. Chert from the Chert Beds has been used by man since prehistoric times to make tools and weapons for hunting. These palaeolithic implements are sometimes found in the Axe Valley Gravels.

Perhaps the most striking features of the coastal section are the outcrops of chalk in the cliffs at Beer Head, Beer Harbour, Pinhay and Whitlands. Inland, the chalk outcrop is limited to isolated patches on hilltops in the Axminster-Seaton area, even though it was once the most geographically extensive stratigraphic unit. Chalk is a very fine grained, pure white limestone composed of tiny fragments of marine shellfish. The chalk was formed from the material which was slowly accumulating and consolidating over a 30-million-year period which ended some 65 million years ago.

Chalk outcrops at Beer

Hooken Cliff

Walking between Branscombe and Beer, one can take either the cliff top route or the coast path into the Hooken Undercliff. This spectacular feature was formed by a landslip one night in 1790, when several million tons of rock slipped down towards the sea, forming the Pinnacles and isolated columns of rock. The resultant cliff face now reveals a full sequence of Cretaceous strata. The weathering effects of wind and rain on rocks of differing hardness has led to sculpting of the surfaces. Fossils are rare in this section, apart from Inoceramus (a bivalve).

From the top of the 425-foot high cliffs at Beer Head, on a clear day the Devonian limestone headlands of Torbay may be seen in the distance westwards beyond the red Permian cliffs at Exmouth.

To the west of Hooken Cliff, an adit from Beer Stone Quarry can be seen emerging onto the face. The 'Beer Stone' is a locally developed hard chalk, occurring up to 15 feet thick, as can be seen in the quarry. This material was used in the construction of churches at Ottery St Mary, Honiton and Axminster and the cathedrals at Norwich and Exeter. The stone, a light honey colour, is soft enough to be easily cut and dressed, but hardens on exposure to air. Quarries have been worked at Beer since Roman times by the method of driving adits underground. Beer Stone Quarry is now worked for agricultural lime only. The old stone quarries are open to the public.

A former quarry at Dunscombe near Salcombe Regis has been reopened to provide stone for the renovation of the south tower of Exeter Cathedral, which has deteriorated over the years. This quarry is worked on a very small scale between September and March. In the area between Branscombe and Beer, there are many small overgrown quarries from which building stone was obtained. Tool-marks may still be seen on some of the bare rock faces.

Flints, which are sometimes seen as nodular seams within the chalk, have been widely used in buildings and walls in parts of east Devon. The flint also gave rise to an old gun-flint industry based on workings in the undercliffs west of Beer Head. These workings were abandoned in the early nineteenth century.

Between Axmouth and Lyme Regis the sequence is complicated by a series of major landslips, especially between Culverhole Point and Lyme Regis, which have been caused by rainwater percolating through the permeable Cretaceous Chalk and Greensand, then running along the impermeable layer of the Gault Clay beneath. Movement of water tends to wash out the lower layers of Greensand, and the lack of support causes the overlying strata to slide seawards.

Early on Christmas morning in 1839, and continuing the following day, an estimated 8 million tons of rock began to slide at Bindon and Dowlands Cliffs, creating a chasm now known as 'Goat Island'. The pressure of the volume of rock displaced upheaved the adjacent sea bed and produced a 43-foot high offshore reef, which ran for about 4000 feet along the coast.

At beach level the walker will become aware of a further change in colour and rock type. The New Red rocks give way to the Jurassic strata. This is the correct sequence in time, but most of east Devon

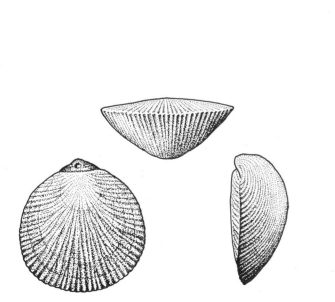
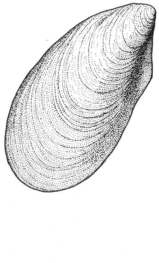

Terebratulina lata (left), *Inoceramus labiatus* (centre), Ammonite: *Mantelliceras sharpei* (right)

was a land surface where no deposition took place. However, Charton Bay marks the shallow western shoreline of the Jurassic sea in which limestones and shales were laid down.

The east Devon coast is not particularly rich in fossils until the Jurassic beds near Lyme Regis are examined. This is the beginning of the section extending into Dorset, where dinosaur and fish remains may be found. Ammonites can be seen densely packed together on the surface of rock platforms on the sea shore.

Localities of particular interest

1. *West Cliff, Budleigh Salterton* (SY 060816) Permian – Triassic. A fine display of the Budleigh Salterton Pebble Beds can be seen in the cliffs, with the Littleham Mudstones to the west. The Pebble Beds are overlain by the Otter Sandstones, which show evidence of aeolian and fluvial deposition. This locality can be approached from Rolle Road at Marine Parade.

2. *Chit Rocks, Sidmouth* (SY 120869) Triassic. The Otter Sandstones can be seen to form a small headland, faulted against the Mercia Mudstones. Access can be gained from West Peak Hill Road.

3. *Beer Stone Quarries, Beer* (SY 215895) Middle Chalk, Cretaceous. A good section through the Turonian, including the Beer Stone, which was quarried out in a series of caves, some of which are still visible. The quarries can be reached via Quarry Lane to the west of Beer.

4. *Hooken Cliff, Beer* (SY 220880) Cretaceous. The section from Branscombe Mouth to Beer Head contains a well-exposed section from the red marls of the Triassic through the whole Cretaceous succession (to the Upper Chalk). The section can be reached either from the beach at Branscombe Mouth (SY 208882) or from the cliff path from Beer (SY 224880). Care should be taken if using the cliff path route from Beer as this entails a long climb down the landslip.

5. *Beer Harbour, Beer* (SY 230891) Cenomanian Limestone – Upper Chalk, Cretaceous. By following the main slipway down on to the beach, then walking south to the first small promontory, the observer will find an incomplete succession of the Cenomanian Limestones which rest on the broken surface of the Upper Greensand. This succession continues all along the southern side of the bay as far as Beer Head. Near the new jetty on the opposite side of the bay, the Inoceramus labiatus Zone is evident, displaying several rhythmically bedded, nodular chalk beds with associated bands of harder material. Along the cliff succession towards the beach huts, a line of flints marks the base of the Terebratulina lata Zone (consisting of massive, marly chalk with a number of courses of black flints). If one takes the cliff path by the beach huts, a clear view up the sequence of soft chalk can be seen. On the cliff path to

Seaton, a prominent tabular flint can be seen at Annis' Knob, which has been taken on the Turonian –Coniacian boundary.

(Note: East Devon District Council has prohibited hammering and specimen collecting in the Beer Harbour area in an attempt to conserve these unique deposits for all to enjoy.)

6. *Whitecliff, Beer* (SY 232892) Cretaceous. This cliff section displays a succession which includes the Foxmould (grey–green sands), Chert Beds and Cenomanian Limestone. Access to this locality can be gained along the beach from Seaton Hole to the north, or from Beer Harbour to the south. In either case, extreme care should be taken to avoid being trapped by the tide.

7. *Shapwick Grange Quarry, Uplyme* (SY 312918) Chert Beds – Middle Chalk, Cretaceous. This quarry is situated along a narrow lane to the north of the A3052, about one and three-quarter miles west of Lyme Regis. This is a working quarry which exhibits Middle Chalk and a reduced succession of the Cenomanian Limestones. Near the entrance there are workings in the upper levels of the Chert Beds.

8. *Pinhay Bay, near Lyme Regis* (SY 320908) Lower Jurassic. This bay is best approached from the Cobb in Lyme Regis. Westwards, past Seven Rock Point, a continuous section through the Lower Jurassic is displayed. Fossils are particularly abundant here, including Plagiostoma giganteum (bivalve), Gryphaea arcuata (bivalve), Calcirhynchia calcaria (brachiopod) and large specimens of Cenoceras (nautiloid). The ammonite fauna is particularly abundant in this section, where very large specimens of Coroniceras conybeari can be found.

A geological code of conduct

In order to minimize the danger when examining rock faces, especially on coastal sections, and to ensure that the localities are conserved for all to enjoy, it is necessary to list a number of points that should be observed at all times.

1. Follow the Country Code and observe local by-laws.
2. Avoid undue disturbance to flora and fauna.
3. On coastal sections, be aware of the tide. Setting out on a falling tide will allow more time. Take notice of any escape routes up the cliffs. The local coastguard service will be able to advise on tide times.
4. Keep away from unstable cliff faces. Remember a dislodged stone might land on someone beneath.
5. Avoid removing *in situ* rocks and fossils. There are often fossils to be found in the debris below rock faces.
6. Always seek prior permission before entering private land. In the case of working quarries, report to the quarry manager on entering and leaving the site.

3 | WILD FLOWERS

The rich variety of habitats produces an abundance of flowering plant species, and a short account can do no more than hint at this profusion. Some of the plants can be found almost all along the coast, others are confined to particular habitats but may occur abundantly there, while some are distinctly rare. The latter should never be picked and, in an area visited by so many people, it is best to leave even the abundant species for others to enjoy.

Although ferns are not flowering plants (they reproduce by spores, not by seeds), a few will be mentioned in the habitats in which they occur.

Shingle beaches

On storm shelves at the foot of cliffs, or on the landward slope of free-standing shingle bars, enough debris collects between the pebbles to form an embryo soil, and a few plants that can withstand high winds and sea spray find a root-hold there. Dark-green leaves of sea beet and neat rosettes of buckshorn plantain can be found throughout the year. Tiny white flowers of Danish scurvygrass appear in early spring, but, in this exposed habitat, most species flower in summer. Portland spurge and hastate orache are interesting rather than showy, but, in the few places where horned poppy grows, its sulphur-yellow flowers and large curved seed pods attract attention. Where there is a little sand among the pebbles, sea rocket and sea kale may be found, and straggly bushes of tamarisk can survive the strong winds where they are backed by cliffs. There is so much bare ground available in this habitat that many casual weeds like sowthistle, groundsel and ragwort appear on it frequently.

Buckshorn plantain

Cliffs

As we saw in Chapter 2, the form that the cliff takes depends very much on the geology. Hard rocks present an almost vertical face to the sea winds, and softer rocks may erode into gullies, which provide some shelter but which are very unstable. The most interesting habitats occur where porous rocks overlie impervious ones so that unstable conditions are produced at the interface; seepage of fresh water at these points creates a flush down the cliffs below the junction, and landslips, recurring over many centuries, have formed slopes of gentler gradient as well as sheltered gullies. In each of these different habitats, a characteristic assemblage of plants may be found.

Cliff faces

Where narrow shelves or small erosion pockets occur, a few hardy plants find a niche. Sea campion is typical of these; it has a long tap root and a spreading rosette of leaves flat on the cliff face so that it can withstand the strongest winds, and its apparently delicate white flowers blow on their flexible stalks without damage. Rock sea spurrey and rock sea lavender provide bright splashes of pink and purple on any kind of rock, but horse-shoe vetch and biting stonecrop form patches of golden yellow on the chalk cliffs only. Rock samphire can grow right down to the base of the cliff, where it must often be drenched with spray, but sea spleenwort, a rare fern, grows only in sheltered crevices and under damp overhangs. A few non-native species – wallflower, stock and red valerian – are completely naturalized in what seems a rather inhospitable habitat, but in fact these south-facing ledges can become very warm, and they provide just the right conditions in which these southern European species can ripen their seed. Bird-nesting ledges, liberally coated with droppings and constantly trampled, may seem an unlikely plant habitat, yet sea mayweed and sea beet flourish there and flower profusely.

Landslip areas

These vary in size, from quite modest slopes not more than a few metres wide at the western end near Salcombe Mouth, to the complicated screes, hummocks and 'chimneys' of the Hooken Landslip and the even more impressive Undercliffs, stretching from the mouth of the Axe to the county border, some of which are virtually inaccessible. The slipped areas consist mainly of alkaline rocks, so lime-loving species predominate, and the unevenness of the terrain in the larger slips provides relatively sheltered conditions, in which shrubs and trees can flourish. Wayfaring tree, dogwood, spindle and wild privet may form a dense scrub; ash can grow to forest size and may be hung with great lianes of clematis and honeysuckle. In the Undercliffs, sea buckthorn contributes a very spiny thicket and box an evergreen one; strawberry tree, with flowers, unripe and ripe fruits all on the same plant at the same time, behaves as if it were completely naturalized there. Another naturalized plant is the green alkanet, a useful dye-plant escaped from the gardens of the cottages which used to be there. In the damp and shade, hart's tongue fern grows abundantly, and typical woodland plants like wood sanicle, moschatel, wood sorrel, ramsons and golden saxifrage flourish. Wherever ivy is found, it may be parasitized by the elegant ivy broomrape.

Not all the landslip areas are scrub-covered; some grassy areas are kept open by rabbits and, in the Undercliffs, by conservation volunteers. Among the grasses, cowslip, primrose and their hybrid, the false oxlip, may be found, as well as blue fleabane, wild mignonette, felwort, early gentian and five different species of orchid. Where the herbage is taller, black mustard, tree mallow and the lovely blue gromwell may be found. Nottingham catchfly, an interesting moth-pollinated species, which smells sweetly at night, can be found almost anywhere east of Dunscombe cliff.

In some places, the landslip areas were carefully terraced to provide small fields on which early potatoes were grown. Donkeys were used to collect seaweed from the beach for fertilizer and also to carry the crops to local markets, where they were much in demand. The springs issuing from the junction of the porous and impervious rocks provided the necessary water, and the warmth of these south-facing terraces ensured an early crop. At Littlecombe Shoot, holiday chalets now occupy these sites but, at other places, the sites are derelict, with a profusion of sedges, grasses, orchids, knapweeds and wild carrot, sometimes with its rare parasite, the carrot broomrape.

Nottingham catchfly

Flush areas

The springs are fed by water that has soaked right through the porous Chalk or Greensand, so they continue to flow throughout the driest summer, and species usually associated with marshes grow there. The tall common reed is a good indicator of where these flushes are, and many tall species like great willowherb, meadowsweet, hemp agrimony, purple loosestrife, teasel and the great horsetail (a relation of the ferns) accompany it. Where the ground is more open, lower-growing species like brookweed, water mint, fleabane, marsh orchid and marsh halleborine may be found. This type of plant may also be found where small streams run down to the sea, as at Salcombe Mouth, Weston Mouth and Branscombe Mouth.

Cliff tops

It is surprising how little salt spray reaches the top of the cliffs, so, along with typical maritime species, many inland plants can flourish there, provided that they can tolerate exposure to strong winds. The kind of soil depends on the underlying rocks, so different types of grassland may be found, and the improved farm pasture may be very different from the natural cliff grassland. Arable fields come close to the cliff top in some places, and the weeds may be very interesting. Woodland and plantation may occur even in quite exposed situations, so each of these habitats will be treated separately.

Heathy grassland

Sandstone usually underlies this habitat, and the soils are thin, poor and acid, often very dry in summer and wet in winter. A large number of typical heath species may be found here, and the following list is by no means exhaustive: ling, bell heather, whortleberry, heath milkwort, heath bedstraw, heath speedwell, heath dog-violet, tormentil, heath groundsel, germander speedwell, common centaury. With this variety of flowers, some of these areas can be very colourful all through the summer. More typical maritime plants like thrift and sea campion are also present, and crow garlic can often be found among the coarse grasses.

Where rabbits occur, they keep the herbage low, and their scratching often produces bare soil. In these areas, very small plants may be found: common whitlow-grass, thale cress, fairy flax, rue-leaved saxifrage, thyme-leaved sandwort, wall speedwell, early forget-me-not and parsley piert. Wild strawberry and barren strawberry often grow together in these places. Both species of gorse may be found, the European or common gorse usually taller and more straggly than the western gorse. The common gorse flowers earlier in

Thrift

the year than the western species, and both are supposed to smell of coconut, but this is usually detectable only on a very warm day. Both species may be parasitized by dodder, the red stems of which wind round the gorse branches like a tangle of red cotton thread. The flowers of dodder are pink, in very noticeable clusters.

Chalk grassland

Like the heath grassland, this can be either tall and rank where it is not grazed by rabbits or sheep, or a close low sward where it is grazed; quite different species are found in each case. The very small plants to look for (often on hands and knees!) in the grazed sward include field madder, spring sedge, hairy violet, carnation sedge, small-flowered buttercup, long-stalked cranesbill and doves-foot cranesbill, thyme, creeping restharrow and chalk eyebright.

A colourful array of taller plants occurs among the coarse grasses of the ungrazed, untrampled areas. These include clary, marjoram, yellow-wort, greater knapweed, field scabious, viper's bugloss, square-stemmed St John's-wort and hound's tongue. The curious burgundy-red flowers of the latter may be overlooked, but the bristly fruits in late summer force themselves onto your attention because they catch on to clothes and dogs' hair and are very difficult to remove.

Orchids may be found, and should never be picked, in an intermediate situation where grasses such as yellow oat grass, sweet vernal grass or quaking grass are not too tall. Orchid seed is very small, and it takes years before a plant is sufficiently established to be able to flower. Common spotted orchid, pyramidal orchid, fragrant orchid and twayblade may be found, along with burnt saxifrage, dyer's greenweed, kidney vetch and musk thistle.

Anthills occur almost anywhere on this grassland, and the fine, well-drained soil that the ants turn up is particularly favoured by some species. Thyme will always be found there, as will bird's foot trefoil, mouse-ear hawkweed, squinancywort, salad burnet and lady's bedstraw.

There are often outcrops of bare chalk, as the chalk soil is so thin, and some plants seem to prefer these conditions. Bee orchid, autumn ladies' tresses, rockrose and the charming little fern called wall rue can be found there.

Well-worn tracks of various kinds can be seen in the chalk grassland. Rabbits use the same way to and from cover and feeding grounds; sheep tend to use definite paths each day, and, of course, we stick to the rights-of-way. Plants with a rosette of leaves close to the ground seem able to cope with this trampling; stemless thistle, hoary plantain and bristly oxtongue are good examples. Another group of species seem to frequent the vicinity of paths although they cannot stand up to trampling; perhaps their seeds are spread along the line of the path. Toadflax, ploughman's spikenard, pale St John's wort, carline thistle, ox-eye daisy, white horehound, knotted hedge parsley and hay-rattle come into this category.

Arable land

Interesting weeds can be found in arable fields, unless weedkiller has been used recently. Common and long-headed poppies, corn spurrey, lesser bugloss, sticky mouse-ear, fumitory, scarlet pimpernel and two species of field speedwell are regular colonizers. Field edges are good places to see weeds such as common mallow, red and white campions and their hybrid, and the slender thistle. The distribution of the latter is interesting, as it is abundant only near the sea.

Hedges

There is often a hedge separating the cliff face from the cliff top, and, as the coastal footpath usually follows this, it is easy to observe the plants of this habitat. The shrubs of the hedge may be hawthorn, blackthorn, bullace, hazel or field maple, but inevitably they will all show the effects of wind pruning, by leaning away from the cliff. The strong sea winds have a drying effect, and this can be felt even through the closely overlapping scales of the buds. Consequently, their delicate tissues are desiccated and killed. This tends to happen on the side nearest the sea more than anywhere else, so the living buds are all on the side away from the sea and grow out in that direction. Certain plants thrive in the shade and protection of these cliff-top hedges. Creeping madder is a climber or scrambler that sometimes almost obscures the shrub it is using for support. Stinking iris, three-cornered leek, goatsbeard (sometimes called Jack-go-to-bed-at-noon because its flowers close up soon after midday, whatever the weather), common gromwell and alexanders are all commonly found here. Common gromwell has very inconspicuous greenish flowers, but, in late summer, the shiny white hard seeds show up very distinctly. Alexanders comes into flower very early in spring and its pollen and nectar are both much sought after

Stinking iris

by insects. Several leguminous plants also tend to be found in this habitat – yellow vetchling, meadow vetchling, narrow-leaved vetch, hairy tare, bush vetch and tufted vetch.

Plantation

On the landward side of a headland, such as High Peak, there is enough shelter from the sea winds for conifers to flourish. Corsican pine grows well and fast by the sea, but here larch and Norway spruce grow well also. Woodland species such as pignut, primrose, dog's mercury and bugle, and ferns such as lady fern, broad buckler, common and scaly male ferns, flourish because of the higher humidity, which is always characteristic of woodland.

Broad-leaved woodland

Although ash is often the predominant tree, the cliff-top woods differ from those in the landslips because the former have been managed as coppice whereas the landslip woods are untouched by man. The ash coppices have a ground flora of bluebells, ramsons, enchanter's nightshade, yellow archangel, wood spurge, wood sedge, wood melick, wood speedwell and even early purple orchids, because the ash casts a light shade and, in any case, is quite late in coming into leaf.

Other woods are of a more mixed nature, often with sycamore predominating. Holly, crab-apple, field maple, elderberry and other small trees or shrubs may be present (including wild gooseberry and tutsan), and the ground flora may include herb robert, wood dock, garlic mustard and the soft shield fern.

Estuaries

The Otter and the Axe both open to the sea by very small mouths because the shingle bar in each case has almost closed off what used to be a wide and open estuary. Salt-marsh, consisting of flowering plants that can tolerate immersion in salt water, has developed in the relatively wave-free conditions, and some of this interesting habitat still remains. However, much of the salt-marsh in each estuary has been reclaimed in previous centuries for agriculture and now consists of freshwater marshes. As the tidal limit in the estuary is reached, the saline influence is reduced and brackish marsh replaces salt-marsh.

Salt-marsh

This is never a showy habitat, many of the plants being a grey–green colour and, after the spring tides that cover the marsh, the plants all have a deposit of silt on them which makes them appear even duller! In the bare tidal mud, glasswort and annual sea blite manage to germinate and produce their fleshy leaves and inconspicuous flowers. Sea purslane fringes the winding creeks which penetrate all sections of the marsh, and sea plantain, sea arrow-grass and sea manna grass make a sward which is very acceptable to grazing swans, geese and duck. Splashes of colour do occur: white flowers of English scurvy-grass in spring, pink clumps of thrift in summer and purplish flowers of sea aster in early autumn. A few plants of common sea lavender may also be seen. *Spartina*, or cord-grass, occurs in the Otter estuary but has not yet spread to the Axe.

Sea clubrush

Brackish marsh

Large reed-beds of the common reed are the first indicators of the decrease in salinity. Sea clubrush and mud-rush often form wide 'meadows', and the large yellow flowering heads of field sow-thistle are conspicuous.

Freshwater marsh

Although the meadows are often intensively grazed, drainage ditches provide good habitats for wetland plants such as wild angelica, hemlock water-dropwort, brooklime and pink water-speedwell. Two colourful garden escapes are to be found: orange balsam and mimulus or monkey-flower.

Casuals

There are often areas of waste ground near the sea – boat yards, car parks, beach huts, informal picnic places, etc. – which provide a habitat for several plants including both natives and garden escapes. Asparagus comes up in the same place year after year, along with fennel and sea radish. The tea plant is a shrub so, once established, it persists for some time. Dwarf mallow, purple toadflax, hoary pepperwort and thorn apple may be seen in the same place for many years and then disappear, to turn up the next year in a different place some distance away.

4 BIRDS

The east Devon coast provides a wide range of habitats for an exceptional variety of birds throughout the year. In spring and early summer the cliffs provide nest sites for certain seabirds, the coastal scrub and woods support a range of breeding songbirds, and the reedbeds and fields at the mouths of the rivers Axe and Otter are a summer haunt for migrants from Africa: swallows, martins and reed and sedge warblers.

In winter these small estuaries attract a wealth of visiting waders and wildfowl. Numbers are not so large as on the nearby and more extensive Exe estuary, but often the birds may be tamer and more approachable on these smaller sites. Spring and autumn bring a further variation in the birdlife, with the arrival and departure of migrants, and the occasional rarity can be found along the cliff tops or on the beaches.

The spectacular scenery of the east Devon coast is dominated by the red sandstone cliffs west of Sidmouth and the chalk cliffs to the east. These cliffs are rather unstable and where landslips have occurred scrub vegetation has often gained a hold and provides food and shelter for many small birds. In spring these cliff-edge scrub areas are filled with the noise of territorial bird song: yellowhammers and linnets in the open scrub areas, willow warbler and chiff-chaff where the trees are taller. Resident birds with territories on these slopes include dunnock, robin, wren, song thrush and many more. Along the cliff top the short grazed areas are landfall for one of the first of the spring arrivals, wheatears, whose white rumps are clearly visible as they fly off when disturbed by walkers.

The steeper cliffs with more stable ledges are chosen as nest sites by larger birds. In particular, between Budleigh Salterton and Sidmouth are some cliffs where these seabirds can find a secure and safe place to breed. Herring gulls are the most widespread along the whole coast, but there are quite a few pairs of their close relative, the lesser black-backed gulls, and a few of the even larger greater black-backed gulls. These noisy and active birds fill the sky alongside the cliff top with their cries, but among them the more observant will find a quieter and more elegant seabird. This is the

Fulmar in flight

fulmar, a member of the petrel family, which flies on stiffly held wings that are used to glide effortlessly in the updraughts at the cliff edge. They nest in crevices, and their attractive clean-looking plumage and tube-like additions to their bills can be seen at close range.

Just to the west of Ladram Bay the cliffs are host to Devon's largest nesting colony of cormorants. (The cormorant is now the

Fulmar on nest

Cormorant

official logo for the Heritage Coast.) These large black diving birds have white throat patches and flanks, which help to distinguish them from the closely related shags, which also nest nearby. More than fifty pairs of cormorants nest, and they can be seen flying along the coast, often forming lines in flight. The smaller shags' nests are more scattered, and in the breeding season the birds have a greenish sheen to their plumage and an obvious crest. They tend to feed out to sea and not to venture into estuaries as regularly as the cormorants.

Many other birds nest on the cliffs, particularly members of the crow family: jackdaws with their ringing calls and grey napes are numerous, but carrion crows and even the occasional pair of ravens can occur. Ravens are best identified by their harsh 'krup' calls and wedge-shaped tails. In early spring they indulge in aerial acrobatics as part of their breeding display, often turning somersaults and tumbling over and over in the sky.

Birds of prey are also found along the cliffs: buzzards and kestrels breed here regularly, and both species make use of cliff breezes to hang in the wind in search of prey. Kestrels are well known for this habit, but in east Devon the much heavier buzzards have become adept as well. Kestrels are often particularly active along the cliff top in late afternoon.

Below the cliffs, on the rocky shoreline the few breeding oystercatchers make their presence known by their loud piping calls and distinctive black-and-white patterned plumage. The other breeding bird of the rocky shore is the rock pipit, a dowdy brown bird with a loud song delivered in parachuting song flight.

Just to the west of Sidmouth the cliffs rise towards Peak Hill. The ridge running inland at this point provides another habitat, that of

Oystercatcher

Female stonechat on gorse

heathland. Inland from the coast road is an area of heather and gorse known as Mutter's Moor. Here a few birds are attracted to the special conditions; on warm evenings the distinctive churring song of the nightjar can be heard. This long-winged summer visitor flies at night in search of moths, but it is sometimes possible to see them hawking low over the heather just before darkness falls.

Tree pipits often utter their flight songs over the heath before landing on the scattered trees, Stonechats are prominent here, the cocks resplendent with black hoods contrasting with rufous breasts as they perch out in the open on gorse or bramble. This area can be host to the occasional Dartford warbler, but these shy and rare birds skulk in the dense gorse and are difficult to spot.

High Peak, at the western end of the cliffs, is the highest point along this stretch of coast, and a pine plantation is just behind on the high ground. The South Devon Coast Path runs through the plantation which, although not rich in birdlife, may have a few species breeding. Goldcrests utter their high-pitched songs, and the repetitive song of coal tits may be heard in spring. The cliff slopes here are well clothed with vegetation and support a good variety of finches and warblers.

The coastal farmland just inland from the cliffs is rather open; it lacks hedgerows and trees and is therefore less attractive for many breeding birds, but the song of the resident skylarks is a continued feature of spring and early summer along the cliff tops. High in the sky, they fill the air with their evocative flight songs. Much scarcer, but also sometimes heard, is the song of the cirl bunting. This scarce bird, a local speciality and a relative of the yellowhammer, is much more common on the continent. In Britain it is now restricted to the south coast, with Devon having the majority of the British population. It is rather more common in south Devon but can occasionally be found in coastal farmland in east Devon. Its song is very like the yellowhammer's but lacks the final phrase.

In places the cliffs are intersected by small valleys running down towards the coast. These sheltered combes, such as Weston Mouth, often have bramble and hawthorn scrub areas with good populations of whitethroats and blackcaps. They are good places to see and hear cuckoos in early spring.

To the east of Axmouth is the Axmouth/Lyme Regis Undercliff National Nature Reserve. The superb undercliff vegetation, with its hanging woodland, provides a rich habitat for birds. Residents, such as robins, blackbirds, song thrush and dunnock, are joined in summer by migrants from further south – blackcaps, garden warblers, chiffchaffs and willow warblers. Treecreeper, nuthatch and woodpeckers, especially green woodpeckers and great spotted woodpeckers, can all occur in the undercliff woodland. Here and there the more open scrub near the cliff-top fields provides nest sites for linnets and stonechats.

Where the cliffs open out to provide views over the sea, herring gulls and occasional greater black-backed gulls can be seen soaring along the cliff face. Below, on the shore line and rocky outcrops at the tide's edge the odd oystercatcher and cormorant can be seen.

At migration times the cliff vegetation can provide shelter for many migrants and a wide variety of birds occur.

Several rivers make their outfall along the east Devon coast: the Otter, the Sid and the Axe. Of these, the Sid is rather small and enters the sea within the town of Sidmouth and thus supports few birds. It is a rather different story as far as the Otter and Axe are concerned. Both rivers enter the sea in wide flat valleys and have shingle bars across their mouths. Behind the beaches are small estuaries with mud-flats and salt-marshes, flanked by grazing meadows and reed-beds. These two estuaries are rich in birdlife, and, because of their relatively small size, they are ideal places to get fairly close to a host of different species.

Winter brings peak bird numbers to the estuaries when wildfowl and wading birds move south from the colder northern breeding grounds. Cold weather movements can bring flocks of birds to these coastal valleys. Lapwings and snipe on the wet meadows, wigeon and teal on the pools and rivers, and thousands of migratory thrushes, redwings and fieldfares from Scandinavia. Severe conditions are not that frequent, but a cold snap can often bring large numbers and the occasional rarity. The regular flock of Canada geese on the Otter estuary in winter can be joined by one or two other geese. It is well worth carefully checking through the flock.

Any winter period will bring a few waders to the mud-flats. Redshank, ringed plover, dunlin and curlew are the more likely, but up to a dozen other species can occur regularly. Handsome black-and-white shelduck are in good evidence on the estuaries, and often a solitary grey heron can be seen waiting silently at the water's edge in search of prey. Herons are a regular feature of both estuaries and can be found in the fields alongside the rivers as well.

In winter it is worth checking the shallow ditches and pools for the shy water rail. This little-seen bird arrives in good numbers on the Devon coast, and some can become fairly tame and regular. The ditches near the footpath alongside the Otter estuary are sometimes a good place to check for them. They often hide in the reeds where their distinctive squealing calls can be heard. Moorhens are frequently seen in the fields, especially near patches of common reeds, and these reed-beds are the winter haunt of wrens and reed buntings. The cock reed buntings have black hoods that contrast strongly with their white moustachial stripes. In some winters the reed-beds have been visited by small flocks of bearded tits; these long-tailed birds have a ringing alarm call, which can help to show their position. They are weak fliers and keep well down in windy weather.

Upstream areas of the rivers Otter and Axe are inhabited by a few other birds. On the water good numbers of mallard and a few little grebes or 'dabchicks', as they are often known, are seen.

Both estuaries have a regular winter flock of gulls. They are mostly black-headed gulls in their winter garb, when only a dark spot behind the eye remains of the dark hood which gives them their name. Others include herring, common and greater black-backed gulls, the last one larger than the others. These flocks can

Herring gull

contain the occasional rare gull, so checking through them thoroughly is a worthwhile exercise. Some rare gulls that have occurred include glaucous and Iceland gulls, Mediterranean gull and little gull.

Kingfishers breed further upstream but winter can bring them down to the mouths of the estuaries where the salinity helps keep the water free of ice. Other special birds to look for just upstream are the grey wagtail, bobbing along the shoreline with colourful lemon-yellow underparts, and, for the fortunate, a glimpse of the dipper. These plump brown birds with white breasts can be found not far inland and are well worth walking upstream to find.

The quietest months on these estuaries are May and June, but often by mid-July returning autumn migrants have begun to appear. Rare migrants have included storks and egrets, and on the River Axe there is always the possibility of a visiting osprey, especially in September.

In winter, one other part of the coast well worth checking is along the rocky outcrops, especially at low tide. Between Budleigh Salterton and Sidmouth there are several rocky areas which are the haunt of shore waders. The larger oystercatchers are joined by smaller but fairly numerous turnstones. These black-and-white waders probe among the crevices in search of morsels of food. A speciality in winter is the purple sandpiper, a wader found only on rocky shores, where it feeds among the swirling waves at the tide's edge but is often surprisingly approachable. Generally grey, the purple sandpiper's yellow legs are a good identification feature.

This chapter has outlined the range of birds that can be found on the east Devon coast. Many others not mentioned can and do occur. It is most important for the conservation of the birdlife that the habitats which attract them are protected. Some parts of the coast are already nature reserves, others are proposed.

All the birds mentioned can be seen from footpaths and beaches with a good pair of binoculars, an essential piece of equipment for anyone interested in birds. Local societies have regular field visits along the east Devon coast. One of the best ways to learn more about the birds is to join the societies and take part in these trips. The relevant societies are: R.S.P.B. Exeter and District Group (Membership Secretary: Mrs R. Martin, Rivendell, Denver Road, Topsham, Exeter EX3 0BS) and the Devon Bird Watching & Preservation Society, East Devon Branch (Mrs E. Brookes, 8 Exmouth Road, Budleigh Salterton).

The range of species will vary depending on the time of year but one thing is certain: on the East Devon Heritage Coast there are always plenty of birds to be seen.

Please take care not to disturb the birdlife, especially in the breeding season. Remember, all wild birds and their eggs are protected by law.

Lesser black-backed gull

5 | THE SEASHORE

Shores along the east Devon coast are favoured with a relatively mild climate, are remote from large centres of population and are bathed by rich waters from the Atlantic, so they can be expected to support a rich marine life, where it can maintain its hold. Much of this shoreline is shingle, which harbours few plants and animals because of the grinding action of the pebbles, but reefs and 'ebbs' of fallen stones provide oases at intervals along the coast, and these form a substrate for organisms that settle from the plankton drifting mainly up-Channel, from the more westerly coasts of Britain as well as from the coasts of mainland Europe.

The most accessible rocky shores on which these organisms can be seen are: (a) Otterton Ledge, approached from Budleigh Salterton; (b) Smallstones Point, near Ladram Bay; and (c) Seaton Hole, adjacent to the town of Seaton. The best estuary and salt-marsh is at the mouth of the River Otter at Budleigh Salterton. The only appreciable stretch of sand is west of Sidmouth, below Windgate Cliff, but it is exposed only at low tide.

Plants of the rocky shores and reefs

Shores such as Otterton Ledge, Smallstones Point and Seaton Hole have reefs with overhangs and crevices, rock pools, which retain water as the tide drops, and turnable stones. Seaweeds mostly grow on the exposed surfaces, unlike the animals which seek the hidden

Zonation of organisms on a near-vertical cliff face below Beer Head: the dark band at upper centre is lichen, the light band below it barnacles and the dark band towards the base of the cliff is seaweed

places and must be searched for. Different weeds occur at different levels on the shore, determined by their tolerance of exposure to the air during the tidal cycle. For instance, the channelled wrack, *Pelvetia*, occurs high on the shore, the spiral wrack, *Fucus spiralis*, a little lower, the serrated wrack, F. *serratus*, at about the level of mean low water, and the kelp or belt-weed, *Laminaria*, at extreme low water. Where there is a run of freshwater over the shore, or where rainwater gathers on the rocks, one tends to find the light-green weed *Enteromorpha*.

In addition to the typical seaweeds that attach to reefs and stones, others, such as coralline algae (*Lithothamnion*), encrust the surface like a veneer, and these pink or purple chalky patches can be seen in pools and on reefs in many places. At Otterton Ledge there is evidence of the occurrence offshore of a most unusual form of this, or a related, calcareous alga, called maerl. The bottoms of pools and hollows on this reef (and only here) contain deposits, not of sand or gravel, but of the dead chalky remains of maerl, and the implication is that there may be a bank of the staghorn-like form of this weed somewhere offshore, the dead fragments coming inshore with the currents.

Two other interesting plants occur on these shores, particularly at Smallstones Point and below Beer Head: first is the sand-binding red weed *Rhodochorton*, which forms a soft, mat-like top to some of the rocks; and second is an example of a plant that is more common in the Mediterranean, the peacock weed, *Padina*, looking like patches of curled parchment.

Shingle beach at Branscombe, with fallen stones of Weston Ebb in middle distance

Encrusting animals of the rocky shore

The sides of every reef and the underneath of every turned rock are populated by encrusting animals, those that are brought to the area as larvae in the plankton and transform as they grow to a form that adheres to the rock surface. The study of this kind of animal makes an excellent introduction to the animal life on a shore, because the common forms can almost always be found and most of them are easily identified.

Turn over a convenient stone low on the shore, peer under an overhang or fold back the curtain of weed on the side of a reef and you should see many of the following.

(a) Small (about 3 mm diameter) white irregularly bent tubes with a sharp point at the open end, which house the filter-feeding polychaete worm *Pomatoceros*; the worm will have withdrawn after disturbance but may emerge again if placed under water.

(b) Tiny (about 2 mm diameter) white neatly spiralled tubes of the polychaete worm *Spirorbis*; again, the food-capturing part of the animal may be seen by leaving the tube under water for a few seconds.

(c) Acorn barnacles, *Chthamalus*, which, underwater, will open the top plates of their shells, protrude their legs and use them to sweep food towards the mouth.

(d) Hard, encrusting sea-mats, such as the bright orange *Umbonula*, in which each tiny animal lives within a chalky compartment less than I mm long.

(e) Soft encrusting sponges, such as the green or cream Breadcrumb Sponge, *Halichondria*, and the orange *Hymeniacidon*, which pump water through their channels to obtain food and oxygen.

(f) Jelly-like sea anemones, such as the Beadlet, *Actinia*, and the purple-green *Anemonia*, which capture food with their stinging tentacles.

The tops of some rocks, especially those not capped by a *Rhodochorton* mat, may have masses of the sandy tubes of the reef-building polychaete worm *Sabellaria*, the openings of the tubes looking like a honeycomb. The softer rocks, such as sandstones that have fallen from the red east Devon cliffs, are regularly bored into by piddocks, such as *Pholas*: live animals will eject a stream of water as you approach, and the shells of dead animals can be seen in old burrows.

Free-living animals in rock-pools

At first sight, one sort of animal seems to dominate rock-pools: marine snails cling to the sides or move slowly over every surface. In east Devon these are mainly top-shells, such as the large *Monodonta* (high on the shore), the striped *Gibbula* (over the entire shore) and the painted top, *Calliostoma* (down towards the low-water line), and they feed on the film of organic matter covering every surface. Also seen in large numbers are the periwinkles, *Littorina*, some living so high on the shore that they are merely splashed by sea water a few times a year, others living in multicoloured profusion on weeds and stones. Across most of the shores will be found the dog-whelk, *Nucella*, with thick, turret-shaped shell, and the sting-winkle, *Ocenebra*, with massive ridges strengthening the shell. These latter two are predators of other shore life, and have special mechanisms for getting at the soft tissues within the shells of barnacles and molluscs.

A rock-pool contains animals that scuttle for shelter as your shadow approaches, but if you remain still and watching, such animals will venture out again. On the water surface there may be groups of tiny blue wingless insects, *Anurida*, which somehow survive in air pockets when the tide is in. In the water itself are shrimps, prawns and shore-dwelling fish, such as blennies and gobies. Any of these may appear to the patient watcher.

As the rocks are turned over, free-living animals will scuttle for shelter. These are chiefly arthropods (jointed-limbed animals), such as porcelain crabs, *Porcellana*, which are cryptic against the rock

A class of adult students working on the shore at Smallstones Point, Ladram Bay

Pinnacles of chalk east of the River Axe

Rockrose

surface when still, small shore-crabs, *Carcinus*, and squat lobsters, *Galathea*. Sometimes a mobile ragworm will wriggle for shelter, such as the green *Eulalia* or the glistening *Glycera*. A brittle-star, *Opiothrix*, may row itself by its arms quickly over the rock surface, and the common starfish, *Asterias*, and the cushion star, *Asterina*, may be seen clinging to the rock with their hydraulic tube-feet. Their relative, the small sea-urchin *Psammechinus* may also be found, holding on by its tube-feet and clutching bits of shell and weed to itself, possibly for extra concealment. The turned stone probably lay on a bed of sandy gravel. When the disturbed silt has settled, you should see small shrimps, *Gammarus*, and tiny light-brown brittle-stars, *Amphipholis*.

The sandy shores

In a stretch like that below Windgate Cliff, Sidmouth, the sand is usually mobile, so does not support a wide range of sand-living organisms. But the sand surface will betray the presence of two common polychaete worms: the lugworm, *Arenicola*, and the sand mason, *Lanice*. The lugworm throws out the familiar cast and the sand mason builds a protruding tube from pieces of shell and gravel topped by a ragged frill of sand-grains stuck one to another, looking like an artist's ill-used brush.

The salt-marshes

The estuary of the River Otter at Budleigh Salterton is an excellent salt-marsh, with a good range of the special plants and animals that manage to live in such a place. Among the plants are glasswort, *Salicornia*, sea-blite, *Sueda*, and sea-purslane, *Halimione*. In the river itself there are animals that can survive exposure to fresh water, such as the ragworm, *Nereis*, young stages of the shore-crab, *Carcinus*, and flat-fish, such as the dab, *Pleuronectes*. In the salt-pans beside the river live huge numbers of the deep-living bivalve, *Scrobicularia*, and the burrowing shrimp, *Corophium*. Under bits of debris may be large numbers of the crustacean *Sphaeroma* which rolls itself, woodlouse-like, into a ball when touched. Everywhere in the waters of river and salt-marsh are the flattened shrimp, *Gammarus*.

The seashore code

If you intend to see for yourself the rich marine life along this coast, please observe the following simple rules, to increase your own pleasure and safety, and to help conserve the wildlife of these rich shores.
1. Know the *time of low water*, so that you can follow down the dropping tide while you study the shore, and are safely off the shore as the tide rises again.
2. *Remove nothing* from the shore, except empty shells where there are plenty.
3. If you turn over a stone to look underneath, always *turn it back again*.
4. Leave no litter, containers or plastic bags behind.

Salt-marsh at the mouth of the River Otter from Limekiln car park

6 | The MAKING of the HISTORIC LANDSCAPE

The 'unspoilt' scenery of east Devon makes it easy for the visitor to forget how much its present-day appearance owes to the efforts of countless generations who have lived here over many thousands of years. The land has been worked by farmers for the last 6500 years and, long before then, prehistoric hunters were exploiting the resoures of the coasts and woodlands. The so-called 'natural beauty' of the landscape is largely made up of a patchwork of farms, fields, woods, hamlets and villages which dates back to the Middle Ages and which still retains elements of prehistoric and Roman life. It is in every sense an historic landscape.

Our understanding of the historic landscape of east Devon depends upon the combined efforts of local historians and archaeologists. The evidence of prehistoric flint scatters and medieval field patterns has to be placed alongside the study of Saxon charters and medieval deeds if the full story of the landscape is to be pieced together. Ecological information and environmental study are also playing an increasing role in helping us understand not just how old the landscape is, but also why it has evolved in the way it has and what life was like in the past.

Our principal aim is to tell the story of the landscape from the earliest prehistoric times to the present century. Archaeology is not just about the oldest sites such as prehistoric barrows. The surviving Second World War defences at Branscombe Mouth* tell us about past efforts to defend this land in just the same way as Blackbury Castle,* a 2500-year-old hill-fort. Victorian farms, such as South Farm,* Otterton (built by Lord Rolle in 1861), are as much a part of our farming heritage as the many medieval farmhouses which can still be seen today.

The message that comes across is one of continuity of settlement. For thousands of years people have put the land to use for farming, defence, industry, religion and other activities, and they will continue this process into the future. This continuity is strikingly shown by excavation which often reveals that a site has been occupied over a long period of time. For example, in Exmouth town centre in 1984 an excavation uncovered strong evidence for Roman occupation as well as remains of the medieval town.

Six thousand years of Seaton

Perhaps the continuity of settlement along the east Devon coast can be demonstrated nowhere better than at Seaton. The Axe estuary is the first major estuary east of the Exe and was a natural harbour location. Although the estuary is now much silted up and reclaimed, it is still possible to stand on Seaton Marshes* and get a good impression of what the estuary used to look like.

The strategic advantage of this estuary, where land and sea routes meet, would have attracted early settlers some 6000 years ago and is the key to the subsequent growth of Seaton. On the eastern side of the Axe stand the massive defences of the prehistoric hill-fort on Hawkesdown Hill, while on the Seaton side a presumed prehistoric settlement called Hanna Ditches is known to have been levelled in the nineteenth century. Another prehistoric earthwork on Seaton Down to the north of the A3052 road may have controlled this early land route across east Devon.

One of the two principal Roman rural settlements at present known in Devon lies on Seaton Down Hill and a series of excavations since its discovery in the nineteenth century has shown that it too occupies an older prehistoric site. Recently it has been suggested that this extensive Roman settlement might have a link with the military occupation of the South-West rather than being purely a villa or agricultural estate. Certainly the possibilities of a good harbour at the terminus of the Foss Way would not have escaped the attention of Roman naval commanders and a stamped tile of the Second Legion Augusta has been found on the site. All in all, the evidence points to Seaton being the focus for extensive prehistoric and Roman settlement. It may even have been the location of the small Roman town of Moridunum which, according to the Antonine Itinerary of the second century A.D., lay 15 miles from Exeter and 36 miles from Dorchester.

We pick up the story again in the Saxon period when Axmouth was the centre of a royal estate and Seaton formed part of another estate called Fleet. The manors of Fleet and Beer are recorded in

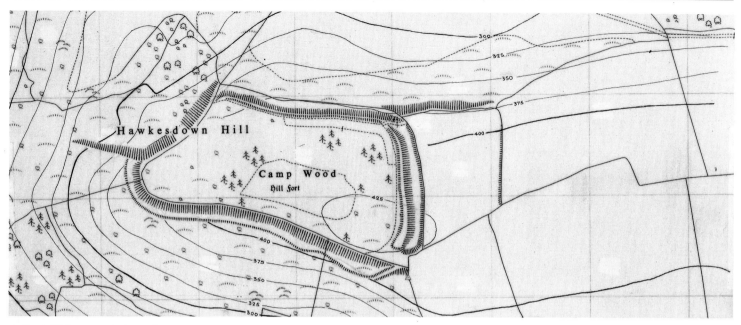

Prehistoric hill-fort on Hawkesdown Hill

Domesday Book of 1086, and by 1146 the place-name of Seaton itself was being documented. The medieval parish church of St Gregory stands in a prominent position overlooking the estuary and the former harbour. Medieval settlement spread along the river-bank to the sea-front. John Leland, writing in about 1540, said that Seaton was once much larger and that its decline was due to the formation of a pebble ridge across the mouth of the Axe, thus channelling the river to the Axmouth side and blocking the harbour. William Stukeley reported in the eighteenth century that local inhabitants 'say there were formerly many great foundations of houses visible nearer the sea than the present town, but now swallowed up'. This again suggests a sizeable medieval settlement with prosperity based not just on the harbour trade and fishing but also on salt-working. Salt was a major industry along the east Devon coast and is recorded as early as 1086. Stukeley saw salt-pans in operation in the eighteenth century and earthwork remains* of the industry (which died out in the last century) can still be seen in the marshes today. Seaton church also contains a gravestone and memorials to salt officers of the early 1700s.

By the 1850s the population of Seaton had recovered from its post-medieval slump to about 800 and its sharp rise to the present-day level of 4980 is due mainly to its position as a holiday and retirement resort, one of the few new industries to make an impact on the landscape since the medieval period. This recent growth has left its own mark with many nineteenth-century structures, and some of these are already becoming a part of the archaeological record. Of particular interest is the Seaton Road Bridge,* designed by Philip Brannon, a London civil engineer. Built in 1877, it was one of the first bridges in the country built entirely of concrete and as such it has been scheduled as an Ancient Monument of National Importance: the youngest Ancient Monument in Devon!

Seaton Road Bridge: this view shows how the concrete has been dressed to give the impression of natural stone

Discoverers of the past

The story of continuity seen at Seaton can be repeated elsewhere along the east Devon coast. We can only touch on some of the main themes in the rest of this chapter, but first we should say something about the people who have helped to put the story together.

We have already mentioned John Leland and William Stukeley, two of the first antiquarians to record archaeological information as they travelled round the country. It was really, however, in the nineteenth century that the antiquarian tradition became firmly established, and east Devon, with its popularity as a health and holiday resort area was, after Dartmoor, the most closely studied area in the county.

James Davidson of Axminster carried out one of the first excavations in East Devon when he opened trenches at Newenham Abbey in the 1820s and a steady stream of chance finds are recorded by writers throughout the century. Many of these came from farming operations (such as ploughing and waste reclamation) or were washed up on the sea-shore. A fine Roman bronze tripod mount of Achilles and a centaur was found by fishermen off Sidmouth in 1840.

Other important finds (now in Exeter Museum) were made by the Reverend Richard Kirwan, Rector of Gittisham, who carried out numerous barrow excavations between 1867 and his death by drowning in 1872. But perhaps the most important local antiquarian was Peter Orlando Hutchinson who lived at Sidmouth from about 1825 until his death in 1897. Hutchinson studied the hill-forts and barrows of the area as well as writing a history of Sidmouth. His illustrated diaries (now in the Devon Record Office in Exeter) contain a wealth of information on the archaeology and history of east Devon.

Many of these nineteenth-century efforts, especially the excavations, fell far short of today's standards. Thus, one of the Rev. Kirwan's excavations began by digging a trench through the middle of a barrow where his workmen thought there might be treasure. A visitor to another barrow excavation in 1868 found a prehistoric cup thrown away on the spoil heap, and, when the British Association visited Farway in the following year, 'so large a slice of the afternoon was consumed at the splendid collation in the tent that there was no time to complete the examination of the barrow.'

Happily the position is different today, with the emphasis on identifying sites so that they can be conserved and where possible made accessible to the public. Archaeological activity now concentrates on non-destructive methods such as field survey and aerial photography. Excavation, an expensive operation, is confined to rescue recording on sites threatened with destruction and to carefully thought-out research programmes.

Over the past half-century important surveys have been carried out by Lady Aileen Fox and by Leslie Grinsell (who has identified more than forty barrows in Farway parish alone). Norman Quinnell and colleagues from the Ordnance Survey have been responsible for adding much to our knowledge as they have revised information for publication on O.S. maps. On the excavation side, pioneering work on Hembury hill-fort north of Honiton was carried out by Dorothy Liddell in the 1930s and this is being added to by Malcolm Todd's current research programme. During the 1960s Sheila Pollard of Sidmouth directed rescue excavations on a number of sites ranging from prehistoric ring cairns to the Neolithic and post-Roman site at Otterton and the Roman villa at Uplyme. More recently Henrietta Quinnell and others have re-examined parts of the Roman site at Seaton.

The 1960s and 1970s have also seen recognition of the importance of historic buildings, especially farmhouses. Public concern at the loss of important buildings has led to the official historic buildings lists being revised, and the survey of east Devon, due to be completed by 1987, is likely to reveal the true significance of our building heritage. Local history has also grown in popularity and Ursula Brighouse's recent parish history of Woodbury is a model which it is hoped others will follow. As we have seen, it is the combination of the archaeological and historical evidence that is so important if we are to discover the whole picture.

The remainder of this chapter will be given over to brief summaries of some of main themes visible in the historic landscape today.

Victorian barrow diggers at work

Farms, fields and villages

The fragile remains of the timber and turf buildings of prehistoric people have been almost completely wiped out. The earliest evidence lies in the heavy stone hand-axes, large numbers of which were found during gravel digging at Broom, north-east of Axminster, in the nineteenth century. These were used by hunters and gatherers, but by the beginning of the fourth millennium B.C. the area was being settled by farmers who cultivated the land on a permanent basis. One site of this date has been excavated on the cliff top at Otterton but otherwise the evidence consists mainly of scatters of flint tools and waste flakes which indicate sites of settlement and other activities. One such concentration has been identified on Mutter's Moor,* west of Sidmouth, but almost every field which has been surveyed on this part of the coast contains some worked flint evidence. This can be explained by the fact that the Beer Head area is the only natural source of nodular flint in the south-west peninsula. Finds from sites throughout the south-west (such as Carn Brea, near Redruth in Cornwall) suggest that Beer flint was being quarried in large quantities and traded over a wide area in the fourth millennium B.C.

Flint is of much less help in identifying sites of the later prehistoric period and our information for farming communities up to the Roman Conquest of A.D. 43 relies heavily on the discovery of enclosures showing as cropmarks on aerial photographs and on excavation results. Work on the Roman sites at Seaton and Uplyme has uncovered remains of pre-Roman round houses and the discovery of a beautiful decorated bronze mirror in a pit at Uplyme shows that this Celtic society was not without refinement. Occasionally sites of this period survive as earthworks; a large area of late-prehistoric fields* can still be seen as banks and lynchets on the cliff top at Beer Head and other sites undoubtedly await discovery.

Stone age tools from Devon. Left to right greenstone axe from Broadclyst, flint axe from Hartland Point, hardstone axe from Silverton (all Neolithic), chert handaxes from Broom (Palaeolithic). Above left Neolithic worked flints of Beer Head flint from east Devon. Above right mesolithic worked flint 'microliths' from Baggy Point

Celtic bronze mirror found at a farm site at Uplyme: this reconstruction, drawn by Philip Compton of the British Museum, shows the intricate pattern on the back

Our knowledge of Roman farming communities is restricted to the sites at Seaton and Uplyme already mentioned and the post-Roman period is even more of a blank. A hint of the probable continuity of settlement comes from Harold Fox's work at Uplyme. He has suggested that the boundaries of the Saxon estate of Lym, which are set out in a charter of King Athelstan dated A.D. 938, correspond to the medieval parish limits for Uplyme. The Uplyme Roman site is located in the middle of this area and it is tempting to speculate that the Saxon boundary represents a former Roman estate. A group of prehistoric barrows on Shapwick Hill may have been used as landmarks in its layout.

With the Domesday Book record of 1086 we can see that the basic pattern of nucleated villages, hamlets and isolated farms was already established 900 years ago. The Domesday entry for Otterton is a good example, describing a farming community complete with market, salt-works and three mills. Harold Fox has shown that villages such as Otterton and Uplyme had their own medieval systems of open fields with subdivided arable strips and even the meadows at Otterton were divided communally into strips marked out by 'merestones'. However, from the fourteenth century the east Devon farming economy began to move sharply from an arable to a pastoral base, with the result that by c. 1600 enclosure had been completed as farmers concentrated on cattle and sheep. It is, however, still possible to see long narrow fields of one or two acres which were originally part of a larger subdivided medieval open field.

The open-field system led to farmhouses being grouped together in village centres. Otterton is again a good example, with several large former farms fronting its streets. However, not all parishes had a nucleated village at their centre. At Branscombe, the houses – several of which are of exceptional interest – are strung out along the valley road rather than grouped around the church.

Beer head from the air: the earthwork remains of prehistoric field banks are visible on the cliff top in the foreground

Defence

The hill-forts of the first millennium B.C. tell us much about Celtic society in the period before the Roman Conquest of A.D. 43. The east Devon area lay across the boundary of two Celtic tribes – the *Dumnonii* of the South-West and the *Durotriges* of Wessex – and east Devon hill-forts such as Hembury,* north of Honiton, have massive defences in the Wessex style. Excavation at Danebury in Hampshire has shown that some hill-forts were marketing centres as well as defensive sites and it may be that the same held true for some of the east Devon sites. In the coastal area good examples can be seen at Woodbury Castle* and Blackbury Castle* and at the lesser enclosure on Berry Cliff*, Branscombe.

Work in Exeter over the past fifteen years has revealed vivid evidence of the Roman legionary fortress that was established on the banks of the Exe in c. A.D. 50–55. We have already seen that the Seaton Roman site may have formed part of the military occupation of the South-West, and the Axe estuary, lying at the end of the Foss Way (the frontier road running across the country from Lincolnshire), was an obvious focal point. Recent work at Hembury* and elsewhere in the area has produced further Roman military evidence.

The cliff-top site at Otterton, which had trading links in c. A.D. 500 with the Mediterranean, is a rare survival of a post-Roman defended settlement, although the place-name evidence of parishes such as Sidbury or Musbury ('bury' being derived from 'burh', meaning fortification) suggests that the hill-forts at Sidbury and Musbury Castles may have been refortified before the Saxon advance in the seventh century A.D. Parts of the modern A3052 are referred to as the 'herepath' or Saxon army road in medieval documents and one of the farms on the road is still known as Harepath Farm. Bindon is documented as the site of a battle between the Saxons and Britons in A.D. 681, after which the Saxon settlement of the area was swiftly completed.

The coastal area contains no medieval defensive sites, but there were some attempts at coastal fortification in post-medieval and modern times, particularly during the Napoleonic Wars. Forts or batteries were erected on the sea-front at Exmouth, Sidmouth and Seaton and a string of pill-boxes, look-outs and other military buildings all along the coastline bear witness to the most recent defence in the Second World War.

Religion

Numerous prehistoric barrows were located on the flat-topped hills of east Devon and the Farway Barrow Cemetery is particularly extensive. Along the coast some barrows may be seen amongst the earthworks on Berry Cliff,* Branscombe, and a prehistoric stone circle ('The Seven Stones') used to stand on Mutter's Moor until the stones were removed in 1830 by Lord Rolle to make a rockery at his

Squat lobster, Galathea

Offshore reef at Ladram Bay (right)

home at Bicton. Another rare discovery was made in the nineteenth century when a Roman burial complete with stone coffin was unearthed near Branscombe. The coffin* is now on display outside the parish church.

Saxon ecclesiastical remains are not common in Devon and the intricately decorated cross* in Colyton church and the crypt* in Sidbury parish church are two important survivals. Medieval parish churches are often taken for granted or ignored but the ones along the coast are well worth visiting. Axmouth church contains some good Norman work, while Branscombe church, with the rare dedication to the Welsh St Winifred who died in *c.* 650, is outstanding.

Industry

People tend to think of the advent of industry as a relatively recent occurrence, but we have already seen that Beer flint was being quarried and traded over a wide area some 5000 years ago. The quarrying tradition has continued with the underground works* at Beer which have recently been opened to the public. Beer stone was first quarried by the Romans and has been found on excavations in Exeter. During the Middle Ages it was extensively used for decorated work in parish churches. Part of the quarry is still working today. The production of lime for agriculture was another important

industry which has left remains along the coast (for example, at Branscombe Humps). Limekilns can still be seen in the car park* at Budleigh Salterton and beside a recent road improvement at Tidwell Mount* to the north of Budleigh Salterton.

The evidence for saltworking has already been briefly touched on, but even more important was the medieval cloth industry. This was a major industry in Devon as a whole and the move away from arable to pastoral farming in the fourteenth century (described above) was due in a large part to the rise of clothmaking. Fulling mills were built in many valleys in east Devon and remains of some survive. It is, however, at the corn mill at Otterton that the best example of a working water-mill can be seen today. The fact that Otterton Mill* probably occupies the site of one of the mills recorded in Domesday Book in 1086 underlines yet again the main theme of continuity which this chapter has sought to bring out.

Sites accessible to the public

Sites marked with an asterisk in this chapter are accessible in whole or part either by public footpaths or because they form part of museum or business premises.

Care should always be taken to leave sites undamaged for future generations to enjoy.

Roman coffin at Branscombe church

Anglo-Saxon cross shaft in Colyton church: the cross fragments were discovered during repairs to the church after a fire in 1933

7 FOLKLORE and LEGEND

'Folklore' and 'legend': two magical words with the power to conjure up visions of supernatural events, strange customs and tales of derring-do; of times gone by, when life was poor but people rich in spirit, when courage and cunning were a man's best weapons, and riches and thrills the rewards he might expect.

It seems strange today to think that the charming, unspoilt town of Budleigh Salterton – a favourite retirement-place of the well-to-do – might have ever been mixed up in any dark doings. But until a century ago Saltern, as the town was once known, was merely a small fishing village within the parish of East Budleigh, or Bodelia. It consisted of a huddle of poor cottages near the sea, and its inhabitants are likely to have divided their activities between fishing and smuggling, for which latter activity this stretch of coast was once notorious.

There were nefarious goings-on at Tidwell, too. Once a manor within the parish of Bodelia, it is today a country-house hotel and restaurant on the road linking Knowle and East Budleigh. Its name is a corruption of 'tide's well' and refers to the hot springs that existed at the front of the house before the land was drained for agriculture. Tidwell was the home of the St Clere family between the fourteenth and seventeenth centuries, and the house suffered greatly at the hands of the last of the St Cleres, Gabriel, who tore it down and sold its timbers and lead roofing, vowing that he would never rest until the house wherein so many sins had been committed had been destroyed. At this time Gabriel St Clere was presumed to be insane, but when a nearby fish-pool was drained shortly after his death the bodies of a man, booted and spurred, and several children were discovered, suggesting that there might have been some foundation to Gabriel's tortured ravings.

In lighter vein, behind Tidwell is an area of woodland that is, according to local folklore, populated by pixies. One lady visitor from Somerset, no stranger to the woods, is convinced that she was

Tidwell House

once pixy-led while walking in the woods. This is a curious pheno-menon whereby walkers who might normally know the way blind-folded find themselves mysteriously walking round and round until totally lost. In the lady's own words: 'I couldn't find my way out, though 'twas there, plain to see. I went all around about it three times, and them somebody coom along to find me and I thought, how could I miss the path. They say others was pixy-led there, too.'

Only a stone's throw from these woods is the village of East Budleigh, where Sir Walter Raleigh was born, and where his father was warden of All Saints Church. Doubtless the young Raleigh would have been familiar with the grave of one Radulphus Node, situated just inside the gate of the churchyard. This unfortunate fellow met his death in the fourteenth century when attempting to fly off the church tower, and the small, weathered headstone which once marked his grave may still be seen against the wall of the clock-tower.

The north part of the churchyard was used for burials only after the 1830s, for it was reputed to be haunted by witches. Although yew trees – symbols of immortality which are believed to protect against all evil – were planted to ward off these nefarious spirits, locals still considered the area to be unhallowed ground, fit only for the interment of illegitimates, felons and suicides. Before 1830 these were buried at Otterton Cross, where it is said that a woman was once burnt at the stake for being a witch.

For many centuries East Budleigh churchyard was used as a meeting-place for villagers, who staged wrestling matches there and played fives against the church tower. During the traditional Ale Feasts, dances and mummers' plays were also performed there.

The old East Budleigh vicarage also saw some unconventional goings-on. Vicarsmead is situated in the lane leading from All Saints Church to Hayes Barton, Raleigh's birthplace, and is one of the oldest vicarages in the country. Its secret passages and hiding-places point to the time when it was used as a meeting-place for smugglers, with the full knowledge and connivance of its incumbents, Matthew Mundy and Ambrose Stapleton, who between them held the living from 1741 to 1852. Their signatures may still be seen, scratched into a pane of glass in one of the vicarage windows.

The Reverend Ambrose Stapleton – the 'smuggling vicar' – seems to have been a colourful character. His sermons could be heard half-way down the street, and his fondness for the smuggled brandy, which he hid in the vicarage and the church, meant that he was frequently the worse for drink. To those who accused him of not conducting himself as a man of the cloth should, he is reputed to have replied: 'I ask you to follow the lantern which lights the way to eternal salvation: I do not ask you to worry about the hand that holds it.'

The vicars' signatures scratched on a window

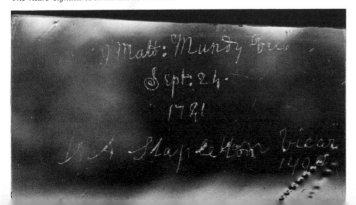

Vicarsmead

Considering its chequered past, it is perhaps not surprising that Vicarsmead had a reputation for being haunted. At the beginning of the century the ghost of a little girl is supposed to have appeared to two sisters who were staying there. She beckoned them to follow and led them downstairs before vanishing. When the slab at the foot of the stairs where the apparition had disappeared was removed, the bones of a child were discovered. They were given a Christian burial, and the ghost was never seen again. It is thought that the child might have heard the smugglers plotting, been discovered, and so met her death at their hands.

The vicarage at Otterton is another that is believed to have been haunted once, but resourceful villagers knew just how to deal with the troublesome spirit. They caused the ghost to be exorcized into a black horse, and then joined forces to drive it over the cliffs at Ladram Bay. The ghost was forbidden to return until it had fashioned a bundle of sand, likewise bound with sand, and even then it could only edge back at a cock's stride a year.

Also at Ladram Bay, near to Sea View farm, is an orchard known as 'Boy-in-the-bush' orchard, for on Twelfth Night locals would gather there for the annual wassailing ceremony. A young lad would be hoisted into the branches of one of the finest-cropping trees to represent the apple-tree spirit, and villagers would dance and sing their homage, chanting:

Here's to thee, old apple tree,
Whence thou may'st bud, and when thou may'st blow!
And whence thou may'st bear apples enow!
Hats full! Caps full!
Bushel – bushel – sacks full!
And my pockets full too, Hurra!

They would then take a liberal supply of cider – often containing toast, wheat-flour cakes or roasted apples – and anoint the roots, trunk and branches of the tree, in the hope that the spirit would be flattered by their attentions and reward their devotions with a bumper crop of apples in the season to come. To make doubly sure, pots would be banged and shots fired to frighten away any malevolent presences.

A little way further along the coast, between Ladram Bay and Sidmouth, lies Mutter's Moor, named after the smuggling Mutter family. Abraham was a turf-cutter and woodsman who supplied Exmouth, Sidmouth and even Exeter with turf cut from his site. He and his brother, Sam, a bold sailor, were in league with the celebrated Jack Rattenbury of Beer, known affectionately as 'Rob Roy of the West' for his daring exploits in organizing the illegal entry of kegs of French brandy all along this stretch of the coast. The kegs were concealed beneath the turf and logs in Abraham Mutter's wagon, a method of transportation that proved so successful that it continued until the coming of the railway did away with the need for it.

Colourful and courageous characters were not confined to the world of smuggling, however. Living on Chit Rocks, in a cottage exposed to the full force of high seas and gales, was the legendary Mrs Partington. On one particularly stormy occasion the sea dared to come flooding into her kitchen, so she rolled up her sleeves, hitched up her skirts and valiantly proceeded to sweep it out. Although she managed to clear one corner, the English Channel did not know when it was beaten and continued to pour in relentlessly.

Equally persistent is another Sidmouth resident, a ghost known locally as 'Talking Kate'. She inhabits one bedroom of a house in the town, and makes her presence known by speaking rapidly over the right shoulder of any guests occupying the room. When they turn, however, there is never anyone there!

Another stubborn ghost was that of one Mr Lyle, who haunted the lower slopes of Salcombe Hill, the site of the Norman Lockyer Observatory, around the middle of the last century. He was determined to make his way towards Sid House, although he could advance only at a cock's stride a year. Six ministers were called upon to exorcize the spirit, but his progress continued unchecked until one day he sat down to dinner with the startled occupants of the house. Deciding that enough was enough, they consulted Mr George Cornish of Paccombe who, despite the failure of the earlier attempts, managed to rid them of their unwelcome guest. Accounting for his success, Mr Cornish explained that whereas the ministers had all been Cambridge graduates he himself was an Oxford man, 'and it takes an Oxford man to lay a really bad ghost'.

Ghosts were not always bringers of bad fortune, however. Legend has it that in 1811 a Salcombe Regis farmer was led by a lady in grey to a hoard of treasure buried on Trow Hill. One of the man's oxen stumbled at the very spot where the apparition had been standing, and upon examination of the ground a large cache was revealed. It was rumoured that as a result the farmer was able to endow each of his many children with £1500, an enormous sum in those days.

Others in Salcombe Regis found wealth not from the ground but from the sea, although the peace and tranquility which surrounds the old church of St Peter makes it difficult to credit that the ancient tower was once a regular hiding-place for contraband. And a little further along the coast, at Branscombe, Berry Barton House is also believed to have been a haunt for smugglers. In the past, the lane serving the farm was often very muddy, so travellers took to the fields on the south side of the hedge instead. There, they occasionally encountered an old woman, dressed in old-style clothing, with a red cloak, and pins in her hair. All too frequently she was to be seen on a style, barring the way. It was believed that she was the ghost of a woman murdered in the house, perhaps because, like the little girl from Vicarsmead, she heard too much. The story was given credence at the beginning of the last century, when bones were dug up in one of the fields, and a little later a stone coffin was found in the same spot.

Another ghost haunts Branscombe, again the victim of a violent death. A woman walking along the road leading from Vicarage Hill to Bovey Cross was startled to recognize a man coming towards her as

Entrance to Bovey House

her husband, for she knew that he had been killed in Italy in 1944. He was dressed as he had been on the day that she first met him, in a raincoat which flapped gently in the breeze. When a motor cycle approached from behind, the ghost vanished into thin air.

As the many ghost stories from this part of the coast suggest, local people believed in and feared the supernatural, something which the 'traders of the night' found very useful. When the last of the

Walrond family passed away in 1786, Bovey House, an Elizabethan mansion now run as an hotel, remained empty for some time. Local smugglers were quick to take advantage of the fact, for it was an ideal rendezvous, and they happily perpetuated the legend that both the house and the lane approaching it were haunted by a headless lady in a blue silk dress. This ghost was officially laid by a bishop in the middle of the last century, but subsequently returned at the permitted rate of a cock's stride a year, and is still to be seen from time to time.

The smugglers who met at Bovey House might have crept stealthily along one of the narrow combes leading inland from Branscombe Mouth; or landed their contraband in a cave cut deep into the high chalk cliff at Beer Head. Perhaps they were guided by a beacon such as the one that Customs Officer John Huxley tried to extinguish in 1755 and met his death in doing so. His epitaph may still be seen in Branscombe Church. Similarly, Seaton Church has a memorial to Midshipman William Henry Paulson, who, with eight members of the crew of H.M.S. *Queen Charlotte*, perished while chasing smugglers off Sidmouth in 1817.

Across the river, Axmouth too had its smugglers' haunt. Stepps House, now a country club, was another favourite meeting-place, and ghosts from the past are also said to murmur of dark deeds perpetrated there. But a weird being of another kind was supposed to inhabit the River Axe itself, for a monster, about five feet long and variously described as hairy, or alternatively as feathery with a tail like a peacock, is reported to have been seen there in the seventeenth century. Twice it is even said to have been seen on the shore, and its last sighting seems to have been in 1644.

Until recently, it was not unusual for visitors to Axmouth to see a goat grazing happily among a herd of cows, for locals were convinced that its presence would counteract the ill-wishing which was held to be the cause of premature calving.

Belief in witchcraft was strong in this area, and a local woman named Charity Perry was greatly feared as a witch. Children even believed that she flew out of her bedroom each night by way of a broken window. One man who fell ill, supposedly as a result of having been overlooked by Charity, was compelled to consult an Exeter white witch, who told him that the old crone would shortly be ill for nine days, and that on the ninth day she would wander up and down the street, weeping bitterly. Charity's reputation was confirmed when everything came to pass just as the white witch had foretold, especially when a neighbour who had nursed her during her illness reported that she had opened a box under the old woman's bed and found it to be full of toads.

Witches, ghosts, smugglers, monsters; dark deeds, dark nights, and the powers of darkness: all are here, in the legends and folklore of this fascinating stretch of coast. The rapt expressions on the faces of the young Raleigh and his cousin as they sit spellbound by the old fisherman's tales in Millais's famous painting, suggest that such legends held the same fascination for our forebears as they do for us today.

Great Seaside, Branscombe

40

The main street at Otterton

8 | SEA and SHIPS

This part of the Devon coast today is a mecca for pleasure-seekers of all ages; off its beaches sail-boarders and dinghy-sailors turn and weave in the sunshine. The area, however, has a maritime history that stretches back two thousand years and there are tales of success and tragedy, all of which have had profound effects on both the people who lived there and on the coastline itself.

Exmouth: 'the best frequented watering place in Devonshire' (Polwhele)

Exmouth, like its neighbour Sidmouth, has links with the sea that date back many centuries. The ferry running across the Exe estuary to Starcross was developed in the twelfth century by Sherborne Abbey, and later acquired by the city of Exeter, though run by the Drake family of Exmouth. Until the nineteenth century it could accommodate coaches and in 1846 was sold to the South Devon Railway. The little port contributed one ship to a naval expedition by Edward I against Scotland in 1298. A much larger contribution was made in 1346 when Exmouth sent ten ships and 193 seamen to join Edward III's fleet against France. In this context 'Exmouth' would have included vessels from Exeter and Topsham as well. Some of the early merchantmen were of fair size; one surviving record tells how the *Christopher* of Exmouth, 300 tons burden, was, with others, captured and burnt by the Spaniards in Bourneuf Bay, Brittany, in August 1375. In 1565 a closer administrative control was established in all ports to make the evasion of customs duties less easy. The Port of Exeter came into existence and included Topsham, Powderham, Dawlish, Lympstone and Kenton as well, all considered to be 'within the river of Exmouth haven'. *Holinshed's Chronicles*,

published in 1577, note of Exmouth: 'Here was sometime a castle: but now the place hath no defence than a barred haven and the inhabitants valour'.

Exmouth probably remained just an 'inconsiderable fishing town' for the next two hundred years, but by the end of the eighteenth century sea bathers had arrived and the population was rising. There was, however, a problem being encountered by those early visitors, as a letter written to the historian Polwhele in 1782 confirms: 'From some of the houses when the tide is in a beautiful view of river, which, united with the sea, forms a fine sheet of water before our doors, of large extent but then its brilliancy is only temporary for, the tide returned, instead of a fine sheet of water, we are presented with a bed of mud, whose perfumes are not equal to those of a bed of roses.' This 'sheet of water', the estuary of the Exe, still provides a haven for yachtsmen and a refuge for wildlife as well.

1782 was also the year when a 'naval battle' was visible from Orcombe Point. Two privateers, one Dutch the other English (modestly described officially as 'the hired armed ship *Defiance*'), met in conflict in Lyme Bay. The English vessel was the victor and the Dutchman was brought into Exmouth harbour as a prize. The bodies of the slain enemy were buried on the Warren at Dawlish 'which the superstitious long believed to be afterwards haunted by their spirits'.

While perhaps less notorious than their neighbours further along the coast, the smugglers of Exmouth were hard at work during the late eighteenth and early nineteenth centuries. The customs boat regularly patrolled the coves east of Exmouth and several large seizures of spirits are recorded, many of the men and vessels arrested coming from Beer. In January 1844 preventive officers seized 'a wagon and four horses, with its driver and several tubs of contraband brandy and *genièvre* [the French word for 'juniper' which provided the flavouring for gin], 50 per cent above proof. They then captured a man carrying two kegs on his back. Proceeding to the beach they seized a boat lying near the shore, containing forty casks filled with fire-water of the same nature.' It was about this time that Richard and Thomas Redway arrived in Exmouth from Dawlish and took over a ropewalk. A street plan of Exmouth shows that this was situated along the north side of the docks, which were completed in 1865. It also shows some unmarked buildings nearby. These may have belonged to Redways who, with two yards, had become both shipbuilders and shipowners and at that time employed a small army of craftsmen and labourers.

Pole Sand, immediately opposite the town on the seaward side of the Warren, has been the scene of many wrecks over the years. This may have prompted Lady Rolle to provide the first lifeboat in 1859. 'This lady also built the boat house at her own expense. The cost of a boat and house was £350,' noted a newspaper of the day. The lifeboat had a coxswain and eight oarsmen but they were unable to help the *Julia* when she was wrecked on the Sand with the loss of six lives in 1867. The men were drowned within sight of those watching powerless on the beach, the lifeboat being 'perfectly helpless to pull against the combined force of the wind and in-rushing tide'. As a result a new and larger boat was sent by the National Life Boat Institution, as it was then known. The R.N.L.I. now stations one of its latest vessels at Exmouth: this is a Brede-type vessel, capable of 20 knots. The force with which the tide ebbs and flows still presents problems and it is often a sharp-eyed user of Exmouth beach who first sees potential danger and alerts the rescue services.

East of the Otter

Domesday Book shows that soon after the arrival of William the Conqueror Otterton had thirty-three salt-workers and in the fifteenth century the export of salt in foreign ships from these saltings was still taking place. From the Middle Ages onwards the river had provided a fair haven for shipping and was a place where ships were built. In 1513 one of the inevitable wars with France broke out and the press gang were out in various parts of Devon, including Otterton and Beer where it is recorded 'ship-wrights and caulkers (the men who stopped up the seams of vessels with oakum and tar) were pressed into the King's Service'. John Leland, the Tudor traveller, visiting this part of east Devon only twenty years later reported that 'less than a hundred yeres sins, ships used this haven but now it is clean barred'. It was then known as Budleigh Haven after neighbouring Budleigh Town (now the inland village of East Budleigh). In spite of efforts to prevent the continuing build-up of this pebble ridge the Otter finally became too silted for any vessels to use early in the nineteenth century. It was at about this time that visitors were beginning to arrive and the pleasant little watering place of Budleigh Salterton developed on the firm ground to the west of that ridge.

Sir Walter Raleigh

If the romantic Victorian painter Sir John Millais is to be believed it was here that Sir Walter Raleigh, the most famous of the Devon 'Sea Dogs', first saw the sea. From High Peak a vast expanse of coastline and sea is seen; in the distance to the south-west is the grey limestone of Berry Head, while to the north-east is the white chalk mass of Beer Head. Further east still is the Dorset coast.

It is a clean cut between land and sea and has been the scene of few shipwrecks in the past two centuries. Today the Royal National Lifeboat Institution maintains just one lifeboat, at Exmouth, to serve east Devon. A hundred years ago lifeboats were sailed or rowed to scenes of wrecks and the R.N.L.I. deemed it necessary to station a lifeboat at Sidmouth as well as at Exmouth. There were then many trading vessels beating courses close to the shore on passage to Exmouth and Teignmouth and small ships were waiting to land cargoes locally as well. Unloading directly on to beaches was common practice in places which lacked proper harbours. This was fraught with danger as the boats were exposed to sudden changes in wind and weather. The vessel would float up on the incoming tide, anchor and then remain high-and-dry when the tide ebbed. The holds could then be unloaded directly into carts or into panniers carried by donkeys. Beaches at Sidmouth, Seaton and Beer were all used in this way.

Lime has been burned to fertilize the land for centuries. There was plenty of limestone in east Devon but a lack of fuel to burn it. Culm, a low-grade coal, was therefore brought from South Wales by sea and landed on these beaches, certainly at Sidmouth and probably elsewhere, then taken inland in panniers to the many kilns in the area.

It was inevitable that from time to time vessels engaged in these activities would be driven ashore when sea conditions changed suddenly. Early nineteenth-century wrecks included the *Samuel* (landing coal), the *Agnes* and the *Amulet*. The decision to station the lifeboat at Sidmouth caused some surprise and at first local people were reluctant to contribute to its maintenance. The

Remington, a thirty-foot ten-oared boat arrived there in September 1869 but it was not launched on service until three years later. One unusual task performed by the *Remington* was the rescue of the Duke and Duchess of Edinburgh who were aboard H.M.S. *Lively's* pinnace when it was hit by a wave near the beach and almost capsized. In 1885 a new ten-oared self-righting lifeboat the *William and Francis* arrived. In 1912, as there had been only one launch to a vessel in distress from Sidmouth since 1883, it was decided to withdraw the lifeboat altogether.

On the day of his adventure the Duke of Edinburgh, as Admiral Superintendent of Naval Reserves, was on his way to inspect the local coastguard station. The coastguard was then administered by the Royal Navy and at about that time John Barber was Chief Officer at Sidmouth where the establishment had a Chief Boatman and fourteen men as well. Nearby, Budleigh Salterton had an officer and ten men also. Both were equipped with rocket and life-saving apparatus. The coastguard passed out of the Navy's control in 1925. It is now administered by the Department of Trade and recent changes in operational procedures mean that there are fewer personnel employed to look out to sea with large powerful binoculars. The Maritime Rescue Sub-Centre at Brixham maintains a twenty-four hour radio surveillance over Lyme Bay and receivers there have the capability to 'fix' potential casualties quickly and accurately. Well-equipped Land Rovers are on regular patrol and can be dispatched to the nearest rescue point when necessary. However, rescues from both sea and cliff have acquired a new dimension in the past decades. Helicopters of the Royal Air Force based at Chivenor and of the Navy at Culdrose and Portland are on call and often perform feats of heroism in the appalling conditions.

Maritime Sidmouth

Sidmouth today is a resort for holiday-makers of all ages and, once a year, the venue for an international folk festival. In former times, however, it had important maritime connections. It has been suggested that there was a harbour in the fourteenth century. Devon ports provided ships for Welsh and Scots wars in the late thirteenth century and in 1301 there is mention of ships being provided from both Sidmouth and Seaton; these were not fighting vessels but were probably small and used only for supply work. In 1318 Sidmouth was instructed, along with Teignmouth and Exmouth, to send as many ships as possible 'to serve for three or four months at their own cost'. The finances of the Exchequer were depleted at the time

Vessel unloading at low tide

Early Sidmouth

and so Edward II's clerks were dispatched to all the ports between Southampton and Falmouth to demand ships at the expense of the burgesses (inhabitants of boroughs with full municipal rights) for the guard of the Channel. Later, in the fifteenth century, an invasion by the armies of Isabella of Spain was thought to be imminent so fleets for the defence of England were again assembled in the Channel and elsewhere. Even fishing boats were called into service but only the larger vessels of over fifty tons actually put to sea. Sidmouth was required to provide three ships and seventy-five men, the same number as Plymouth.

In the early seventeenth century the old enemy across the Channel was again causing trouble. In June 1628 the Deputy Lieutenant-Governor of Devon felt it necessary to write to the Earl of Bedford 'praying him to move the Privy Council that some fort be erected at Sidmouth at the charge of the country'. He was told that 'the Frenchmen do hover upon our coasts and have done much spoil. Our fishermen are afraid to go to sea, and the writer fears their landing to burn our towns.' The Earl dutifully passed the request to the Lord President but no action seems to have been taken. It was about this time that Devon was being troubled with pirates as well, 'both Dunkirkers and those of our own natives', that latter being of course renegade Englishmen. They must have been cruising off east Devon during the 1620s as the Account Book of Sir John Eliot, Vice-Admiral of Devon, records the sale of 'two hogsheads of white wine [taken and] landed at Sidmouth from piratts'.

It was also at Sidmouth that the most recent efforts were made to provide a harbour on this part of the east Devon coast. Money was subscribed for several ill-conceived projects, all of which failed with consequent financial losses to the participants. The most recent of these was only seventy years ago. It was lack of shelter that caused the total loss of the *Duchess of Devonshire* in 1934. This

well-known paddle-steamer regularly disembarked her day-trip passengers on various south Devon beaches, using a ramp lowered by a derrick on the bow, in a similar way to that used on assault landing-craft in the Second World War. She was completing this operation on Sidmouth beach when a wave lifted her stern and drove her ashore broadside-on.

Duchess of Devonshire

Branscombe, a smuggler's paradise

The romantic aspects of former smuggling days were still fresh in the memory less than a century ago. 'Until the lowering of duties made cargo-running unprofitable, the peasantry all along the shore were greatly demoralised by smuggling. A very cursory examination of the cliffs shoreward will shew how numerous were the paths and byways over which a band of men might easily transport their small "kegs". The large luggers of Beer were chiefly employed; from their size there was little risk in crossing the channel. Numberless were the tales told by a former generation of steep ascents which no man would have faced by day, of false alarms, of devices for drawing away or deceiving the preventive men.' Hollow ledges, holes excavated in the sides of wells, sinking kegs at sea were common hiding places. The subterfuges were not always successful. On 3 November 1827 the Revenue cutter *Nimble* captured and took into Exmouth a smuggling boat with 135 casks of spirits aboard. It had a crew of two Frenchmen and 'three belonging to Beer'. This was

Jack Rattenbury

probably intended to be landed as a single operation or 'run' and it gives some idea of the scale of smuggling going on. On occasions one of the incumbents of Branscombe embellished his burials register with biographical notes. When he buried William Cawley in 1801 he wrote revealingly that 'he had been on a smuggling expedition and was found dead early in the morning by John Halse in a field of oats called Five-Acres, lying on his back with his head down hill and [a] cask of spirit at some distance from him.'

There is also a memorial to an upholder of law and order. John Harley, Customs House Officer at Branscombe, 'fell by some means or other from the top of the cliff to the bottom, by which he was unfortunately killed'. He was attempting to extinguish a fire on the cliffs which was a signal to a local smuggling boat. His epitaph ends 'he was an active and diligent officer and very inoffensive in his life and conversation'. The smugglers were in reality ruthless and cruel; many honest men, in particular members of the Revenue Service, were murdered or badly injured by them. Jack Rattenbury, the most notorious of them all, retired into respectability in his old age and wrote his autobiography. He was born in Beer and became known as 'Rob Roy of the West'. Many Beer men were engaged in the smuggling trade. Their boats were famous for their seaworthiness and their chances of surviving in stormy weather were enhanced when 'these daring rascals lashed their tubs together as a sort of breakwater around their boats'.

It is of course from fishing that the people of Beer have made their living over the centuries. About ninety years ago seining was still possible. Some years before that a huer would be on watch all day during the season and if a shoal of mackerel began to 'play' (spring out of water), the valleys would echo to the watchman's cry of 'a haul' as it was passed from person to person. The boats were ready to be launched and if all went well the great net was cast overboard and the fish surrounded. When drawn ashore, catches of 'one, five or even ten thousand glittering prisoners' were not unusual. The Branscombe register describes in full detail the tragic demise of Edward Hurley in 1795. Despite the fact that 'the several means recommended by the Humane Society for the recovery of drowned persons were used for several hours', all attempts at resuscitation were in vain and 'he was thus in an awful moment, launched out of time in [to] Eternity'.

West of Lyme

It has been widely recorded that the estuary of the Axe may have been chosen by the Romans as the southern terminus of the Foss Way, their great military and trade route across England. It was then probably one of the finest and most extensive harbours on the south coast, stretching from the Burrow at Seaton to Haven Cliff, perhaps then more than half a mile wide and extending up the vale for four and a half miles. The Romans improved communications in the area and it is purported that cargoes such as iron from the Mendips and wool from the Cotswolds were shipped from here. More recently, however, it has been explained that although Ptolemy's map indicates that it is a fair assumption to place the terminus of the Foss Way at Axmouth it would be expected that the name would be derived from Isca. As the prefix 'Ax' was established by the ninth century A.D. and in view of the present lack of archaeological finds and other evidence of Roman occupation there (except for the villa at Seaton), a positive location cannot be determined. The haven was still in use when a Danish prince landed there in 957. However, indications are that, following a major landslip at Haven Cliff soon after the Norman conquest, the mouth of the Axe became blocked as the tides piled up shingle against the fallen rock.

By the fifteenth century there were obvious problems because in 1450 Bishop Lacy of Exeter granted forty days indulgence to true penitents who contributed to the 'reparaction of a haven at this place'. A century later when Leland viewed the scene he recorded, 'Ther have been a very notable Haven at Seton but now ther lyith between the 2 Pointes a mighty Rigge and Barre of Pible stones'.

Later, through Acts of Parliament passed in 1792 and 1820, attempts were made to replace an unfinished pier which had been washed away in a 'great tempest' two centuries earlier, but both failed. The last topsail schooner anchored by the inn at Axmouth more than a hundred years ago and the building of the bridge in 1877 probably ended all trade from the ancient port. Consequently both Beer and Seaton across the Bay retain their relatively unspoilt beauty.

The great landslip east of the Axe changed the shape of the coastline but had little effect on the economy of the district. East Devon people were, however, much involved when James, Duke of Monmouth, landed at Lyme Regis just over the boundary in Dorset in 1685 and attempted to raise a Protestant insurrection against James II. His untrained forces were soon defeated at Sedgemoor.

Many were local men from parishes in the neighbourhood and some suffered the ultimate penalty of being hung, drawn and quartered at the callous hands of Lord Chief Justice Jeffreys.

The future

The creation of the Heritage Coast ensures that in future lovers of both land and sea will be secure in the knowledge that there will be little further 'destruction at the hands of the despoilers' and that any changes in the seascape will be made by nature rather than by the hands of men.

Schooner

Fishing boat from Beer taking tourists on a pleasure trip

48

Harvesting on the cliff top

9 TRADITIONAL BUILDINGS

From the Exe estuary to Lyme Regis, the most spectacular sights are not of man's making but the cliffs and headlands that rise sheer from the sea. From the cliff tops near Sidmouth which are 500 feet high it is possible to see Berry Head in the west and Portland to the east. The vivid red sandstones of Sidmouth's cliffs contrast with the white chalky cliffs around Branscombe and Beer, which are equally precipitous. Whilst the cliff scenery is spectacular, the landslip area between Seaton and Lyme Regis is intriguing and secretive. Here the Coast Path wriggles beneath a forest canopy which is fully mature after almost 150 years. Within the folds of hills and in hidden valleys and sometimes spilling along a combe to the seaside are several attractive towns and villages. Each has some church or barn, house or bridge, which echoes bygone days with charm and with qualities never recaptured by new ones. These buildings are the milestones of time, capturing the history and prosperity of places in their fabric and styles, showing past endeavours and investment that still bear fruit today. In their way they are as remarkable as the countryside that surrounds them.

Exmouth is the oldest seaside resort in Devon. It grew from a mere collection of fishermen's huts to become a haven for those who were ill and needed the fresh and invigorating sea breezes to restore them to health, or at least to give them a chance to enjoy ill health. By the end of the eighteenth century it was considered, 'during the Summer months, an eligible retreat for the children of idleness and gaity', and the luxurious and attractive houses of the Beacon, together with other adjoining roads around Bicton Place, were built in the late 1790s. Here Lady Nelson lived in comfort at No. 6 and Lady Byron at No. 19, enjoying the sands of Exmouth as well as the company of neighbours of quality at the turn of the eighteenth century.

This Georgian splendour still dominates the heights above Exmouth's sea front, although nearer the harbour the Victorian terraces have their own ornate appeal. Exmouth harbour is capable of taking small coasters and sheltering a good number of pleasure

No. 19 The Beacon, Exmouth

craft and is close to the estuary mouth. The bustle of the docks and movement of ships is always fascinating, and the rows of small Victorian terraces are not unlike many built in those industrious times.

Eastwards of the harbour, towards Foxholes, lies the cricket ground which supports the atmosphere of lazy idyllic days in a pleasantly frolicsome old-fashioned holiday resort where gulls scream and saucy postcards are sold together with the inevitable pink coloured rock. While the elegant Georgian buildings and ornate and imposing Victorian ones are repeated elsewhere along the east Devon coast, the Barn, on Foxhole Hill, designed by E. S. Prior, a pupil of the well-known architect Norman Shaw, and built in 1897, is quite unique. Art Nouveau design in Devon is not plentiful, and this building, originally a house and now a small hotel, is striking in its use of stonework and massive round chimneys.

The Coast Path starts just below the house and skirts the rear gardens of more modern comfortably traditional houses. This stretch of the coast, as far as Budleigh Salterton, guarded once, it seems, by a single derelict pillbox now used more peaceably, is not the most attractive, although pleasant enough, with views back over the rough common of the Maer and Exmouth to the Exe estuary or seawards over Lyme Bay.

Budleigh Salterton, a quietly fashionably resort where Sir John Millais painted his famous 'The Boyhood of Raleigh' at the Octagon, lies at the mouth of the Otter estuary and it is here that the East Devon Heritage Coast begins. High Street and Fore Street have a pleasant stream flowing beside them, and are fronted not only by shops but also by early Victorian villas with bridges spanning the stream. One of these pleasant buildings has been used to house the local museum – The Fairlynch Art Centre and Museum – where there is an interesting collection of local exhibits. There are a number of splendid early Victorian houses, often using the Gothic style so commonly adopted in the first fifty years of the nineteenth century, with spacious gardens, mature trees and shrubs. They, above all

No. 6 The Beacon, Exmouth

else, contribute to the spaciousness and feeling of gentility that is evident here. Many of the properties are relatively modern, although some small cottages and farmhouses built of cob and thatch are left from the time when farming and fishing sustained a smaller community.

Nearby are the villages of East Budleigh and Otterton. Both are picturesque and the cob and thatched cottages in East Budleigh's main street are a remarkable testimony to the durability of sixteenth- and seventeenth-century craftsmanship and the local red clay and short chopped straw that make cob walls. White rendered, with a thin cobbled margin to the road, they present a picture-postcard appearance, more attractive because of the sparkling brook that flows through the village. The largely fifteenth-century red sandstone church of All Saints, which stands at the higher end of the main street is a church of bosses and deep-carved bench-ends. Most, like that of the Raleigh family pew, with the crest and a date of 1537, were carved about 400 years ago. Two modern bench-ends commemorate the First World War.

A visit to Hayes Barton Farm, a beautiful Tudor mansion half a mile away, is worthwhile. It retains the charming style of Elizabeth I, with the thatched and gabled roof, mullioned windows and projecting porch. Sir Walter Raleigh was born here in 1552 and his adventurous career has added historic lustre to a quiet and unassuming village.

The Octagon, Budleigh Salterton

It is not more than a mile and a half from the northern edge of East Budleigh to Otterton. As one turns off the main road to Otterton at the crossroads about half a mile from the village, there is visible nearby a grey stone obelisk erected in 1730 as an 'eye catcher' on the Rolle Estate when the mansion of Bicton was built. This magnificent mansion is used as an agricultural college, although the picturesque gardens, originally laid out by André Le Nôtre (who designed the gardens of Versailles) for the benefit of Lord Rolle, are open to members of the public, and sport a miniature railway for children. The fine parkland and pinetum are likely to be preserved in the way they were intended, with what was once a fine stately home maintained in its planned setting. The entrance is a quarter of a mile beyond the crossroads on the Newton Poppleford Road. However, to reach Otterton it is necessary to turn right at the crossroads which are marked by an ancient red brick pillar, dated 1743, with a stone cross on top. Recently the text carved on the stone plinth beneath the cross has been renovated with the help of the Otter Valley Association.

A short distance along this road is what was formerly a bridge over the Tiverton Junction to Budleigh Salterton branch railway, built in 1897, and recently dismantled. A neatly converted railway station and brick bridge over the lost railway remain as a tribute to the steam engines that once hissed their way to Budleigh Salterton and Exmouth. Beyond is another finer bridge, in stone, with three wide arches that span the River Otter. Since the eighteenth century, when an earlier bridge was replaced, it has been a splendid approach to Otterton.

The old mill close to the river is now a craft centre where one may buy pottery or furniture made on the premises by craftsmen. The wide main street has a stream running beside it which is crossed by a number of foot-bridges. It is lined with rows of white rendered cottages that seem to have remained largely unspoilt since the time that many of them were built in the sixteenth and seventeenth centuries. Some of the most ancient have enormous chimney stacks standing proud of their walls, probably added in the seventeenth century as part of the modernization work common at this time. It was the practice to remove a central open fire which burnt in an open hall and to provide additional space by putting in ceiling beams and floors and cutting dormer windows into the lower part of the roof. But like all fashions it was much copied and an external chimney stack was often provided for new houses built at this time. The appearance of the main street, which takes up most of the village, is a little deceptive since here and there modern houses have been built, generally with unobtrusive good manners. Thanks to this the ancient cottages and farmhouses remain pre-eminent and, like Basclose Farm with its chimney dated 1627, hint at quieter Tudor times, when this was a remote fishing village.

Between the valleys of the Otter and the Sid lies a band of rich arable land crisscrossed by typical Devon lanes, narrow and high-banked. The descent to Sidmouth is both sudden and breathtaking. From Peak Hill it is possible to enjoy panoramic views along the

Basclose Farm, Otterton (left)

Otterton main street (below)

The Esplanade, Sidmouth

Alma Terrace, Sidmouth

coast and look down on Sidmouth, sprawling along the River Sid, dominated by the woods and green hillsides of this wide valley. This is a town of elegance, worth whatever time that can be spared to explore and enjoy the abundant Regency architecture. Self-contained detached villas were often built on eminences, each surrounded by ample gardens which have now matured and whose trees and shrubs provide an attractive setting for many of them. The sudden popularity of Sidmouth, and of Exmouth, at that time arose from the restrictions placed on travel abroad by the Napoleonic wars, which forced the aristocratic and wealthy to explore elsewhere. The expansion of the railways in the 1840s also helped the growth of the town. Moreover, it coincided with a time when one of the most gracious and well-ordered forms of architecture was in fashion, and wealthy patrons could afford to pay.

Whatever changes have taken place, the town remains a monument to Regency times. Fortfield Terrace, built between 1792 and 1800, was not completed, but its scale and order help to disguise this defect. The double-headed eagle in the central pediment commemorates the stay (at No. 8 in 1831) of the Grand Duchess Helen of Russia. Clifton Place, York Terrace, The Esplanade, Amyatts Terrace, Alma and Cambridge Terraces, are all finely preserved and impressive and characteristic of this period when Sidmouth grew rapidly. So too are the individual houses like Audley or the Royal Glen Hotel (once known as Woolbrook Glen and visited by the Duke and Duchess of Kent in 1819 with their infant daughter, later to be Queen Victoria) and it is the spaciousness and elegance maintained in places like Elysian Fields that impress the visitor. They provide an opulence which only a bygone age of inequality could have produced. The romantic grandeur displayed by Woodlands Hotel, created to satisfy Lord Gwydir's demand for a cottage, was repeated many times on prominent sites in and near the town

Woodlands Hotel, Sidmouth

for others. The Gothic idiom, stucco and thatch clearly announced the superiority of Sidmouth.

So it remains today, in spite of the Victorian terraces and inter-war semi-detached houses, which spread up the valley and threaten to engulf Sidford. Sidmouth still has its share of ancient cottages, already old in Regency times, the homes of farmers and fishermen. Renovations of Tudor Cottage, in Chapel Street, uncovered wall paintings from Henry VII's time, justifying its name. A stroll through the Byes up to Sidford will be rewarded by seeing a similarly ancient row of thatched cottages. Just as interesting is the ancient stone hump-backed pannier bridge over the River Sid at the bottom of the hill towards Salcombe Regis, and incorporated into a more modern one needed for the heavy traffic on the A3052.

Immediately to the east of Sidmouth is Salcombe Regis, easily approached up a south-facing combe. This is possibly the smallest village along the coast. It is remarkably pleasant; even the church car park and sitting area is delightfully planted, attracting numerous butterflies on bright summer days. St Peter's Church, which is the centre of this village of slated and white-walled buildings, dates from the twelfth century and is one of the finest medieval churches in the county.

St Peter's Church, Salcombe Regis

In 1939 a stone was placed on the site of the ancient pound, on the north side of the village, to commemorate the planting of a new thorn tree, a plant used continuously since Saxon times to mark the parish boundary and the boundary between the cultivated land of the combe and the open common of the hill. Adjacent to it is the old thatched farmstead of Thorn where the Manor Court was held in Elizabethan times, and at nearby Dunscombe the remains of a former mansion may be seen.

Flint rubble walls are common in Salcombe Regis and although the use of flints in buildings at Otterton and elsewhere along this part of the coast is far from rare, here it contributes to the harmony of the place, whose buildings are themselves well matched in scale and materials. The Victorian village school, built of knapped flints, has been converted to a house and this is one of the obvious signs of the times, but the presence of farms in the very centre of the village is proof of the unchanging reliance of the community on agriculture, although this does not prevent Northcombe farm serving teas to tourists in the most amenable setting.

Between Salcombe Regis and Branscombe lies the hamlet of Weston, a collection of old farmhouses at the head of the combe. Here, the elegant eighteenth-century house of the Stuckeys stood, until it was destroyed by a disastrous fire. All that remains today is part of the shell of the house and the gate piers.

Branscombe and Beer, like Salcombe Regis, have relied in the past on reaping harvests on land and sea. As at most other attractive spots in east Devon, tourists and retired people contribute to the economy now. At Branscombe three valleys join and tumbling streams from each meet and flow into the sea at Branscombe Mouth. From here, extensive views across Lyme Bay may be enjoyed, on clear days to Torbay and Berry Head away to the west and to the east even further to Chesil Beach and Portland Bill.

Branscombe must have one of the most attractive settings of any village in Devon. Unlike other villages, it straggles along valley roads. Three separate groups of buildings have particular importance, although away from them other houses and small thatched cottages settle into the sides of hills to shelter from the winter rains and winds. The largest group is about half a mile up the valley from the shingle beach at Branscombe Mouth, and the older grey stone and slate properties jumbled along the roads converge at the Mason's Arms, which, like so many ancient pubs with a reputation for good food, is most attractive. Some of the more modern houses have been built to reflect the colours and materials of the fishermen's cottages which have weathered and changed over the last 300 years, and generally do so with some success.

Up the valley, near the village hall, are two or three attractive thatched buildings. One is the village bakery, run by Collier & Sons, who still use faggots – bundles of brushwood – to fire their ovens. The rare sight of a long low pile of these bundles can be seen close to the bakehouse cottage. On the other side of the road is a smithy that produces horse shoes, as well as mementoes for the tourist trade. These ancient crafts carried out in equally ancient premises are a bonus for the inquisitive or romantic who value good quality. Close by is the church of St Winifred and opposite an attractive sixteenth-century house called Church Living. Professor W. G. Hoskins has described St Winifred's as 'being one of the most "atmospheric" churches in Devon of the highest interest, for it exhibits a process of continuous development from the 11th to the 16th century'. He suggests that 'the massive central tower and part of the nave are Norman; the transepts and west half of the nave 13th century; and the chancel early 14th century'. The fervour and beliefs of earlier times are often displayed on tombstones like that of Charity Lee close by the church door.

Here lyeth entond the remains of
CHARITY LEE
with her only husband WILLIAM LEE and her only son ROBERT LEE. Was after almost fivety years most exemplary widowhood with public lamentation and firm hope of a future resurrection to eternal glory departed this life on the 10th day of April 1709. Aged 94 years.

Margells, Branscombe

St Winifred's Church, Branscombe

Hole House, Branscombe

The third of the larger groups of stone and thatch buildings, more than a mile from the first, is just as old. In one of the cottages, now owned by the Landmark Trust, painted walls of the sixteenth century were discovered.

Outside these three main groups of buildings stand some impressive houses in the countryside. Near Branscombe Mouth, where local crabs are sold, is Great Seaside which, with its imposing chimney, seems to be Elizabethan. Alongside stands an unusual walnut tree. To the north of the parish is Edge Barton, the home of the Branscombs until the reign of Edward III. The Wadhams, a family associated with the Oxford College, followed them. Hole House and Barnells are of considerable antiquity. The present house at Hole is largely sixteenth century, although Hole was recorded in the thirteenth century and was the home of the Holcombes until the seventeenth century. Bovey House, an Eliza-bethan mansion, contains some outstanding seventeenth-century

plaster work and was once the home of the Walronds. It is now a hotel and has the distinction of being haunted. A nearby well is so deep that buckets of water were retrieved by use of a treadmill, which gave many generations of small boys great exercise.

The most westerly outcrop of chalk in the country is around Beer and Branscombe, and from this outcrop the famous Beer stone has been quarried since Roman times. It was used by medieval craftsmen in Exeter Cathedral, and today stone is taken from the same quarries for the Cathedral's repair. Today the stone is worked from an open face and often burnt in a coal-fired kiln for agricultural use. Countless farmhouses and churches have incorporated this easily carved white stone, and in Beer it features widely in the older buildings. Knapped flint was equally popular for building. While the village may not be as picturesque as some, its beach is crowded with small fishing boats, lobster pots and nets being prepared for use, a sight seen here for centuries. To buy local dabs

The main street, Axmouth

and herring from the beach could hardly be more fitting.

Seaton is a substantial town with plenty of shops to satisfy its many holiday-makers. There are few interesting or ancient buildings here, the town being mainly of the late-Victorian and Edwardian eras. However, the small harbour is a constant source of interest and the marshes of the River Axe are the meeting-place of many different birds, including curlews, turnstones, oystercatchers, lapwings and redshank.

Axmouth is picturesque and can be reached from Seaton by taking the road past the harbour and over the bridge and then northward beside the estuary. Dominated by the ancient hill-fort of Hawkesdown, this attractive little village contains several good Elizabethan stone farmhouses. St Michael's Church, like St Winifred's of Branscombe, has a long history dating back to Norman times.

About half a mile north of the village, Stedcombe, a manor house built in 1695, presents an apparently unchanged appearance in unspoilt countryside. Built in the Queen Anne style, with bricks and stone quoins, it was a fine country gentleman's house.

Beyond Seaton the Coast Path passes through the tangled woodland of the landslip area, free from any settlements or farms, although old walls, all tumbled down, can be discovered in the undergrowth. Away from the coast there are some old farmhouses and buildings, but only Rousdon mansion, built in about 1870 of stone and brick for Sir A. W. Peek, is notable. Since 1937 it has been used by Allhallows School, and, while it still reflects Victorian romantic tastes and was intended to capture the feeling of Tudor times, it has little historic interest.

The unparalleled scenery of this part of the coast, which has become romantically linked with John Fowles' novel, *The French Lieutenant's Woman*, is outstanding. Much of the novel's action is in Lyme Regis, the first town in Dorset and a splendid introduction to the pleasure of the Dorset coast.

10 TRADITIONAL INDUSTRIES

East Devon has one of the mildest stretches of coast in southern England – it is even milder than the Loire valley – and people have lived here and set up industries for their needs since the Neolithic period. At that time the black flints from Beer Head were produced on a scale which made them exportable, and their use continued until the days of the Roman villa on Seaton Down. There was no reason for the local people, who knew how to make axe and hammer heads, to stop using flints. The same has been true of other industries, such as boat-building. Fishing boats have been clinker-built from traditional materials for many hundreds of years, and they are still made to the same design as when they were powered by sail.

It is natural, since we are considering the coastal strip, to think about industries connected with the sea. There is a series of small inlets and harbours with steep shingle beaches between Budleigh Salterton and Lyme Regis and each river mouth has its fishing villages and towns. The nature of the small eroded valleys, and the hills between them, means that the coastal settlements are self-contained, even in the crowded summers. Boats are often family-owned, and some families combine fishing with running a fish shop in the town. Crabbing and lobster fishing are still done traditionally with pots and nets, and at Beer the catch is sold live from a great tank on the beach. Nets are made now by machine at Bridport, but fishermen still learn the skill of net-making so that they can mend their nets on the cold winter days when fishing is impossible. Some learn from their fathers, others go to courses run by the Deep-Sea Fishermen's Association.

One family firm at Seaton makes clinker-built fishing boats. Clinker-building dates back to the Viking period when boats were built by overlapping the planks of a boat and rivetting them through. This gives great flexibility in our northern seas, as well as strength. The boats made at Seaton have been designed to be easy to winch up the steep pebble beaches of the district, and are called beach boats. Their timbers, which are local, are heavier than usual; ribs and frames are of oak and the planking is elm. Copper rivets are used. They are sent all over the country to places as far apart as Hastings, Aberystwyth and Lake Windermere. East Devon fishermen like to replace their beach boats every fifteen or twenty years because of the battering the boats get when they are launched down greasy timbers to the sea from the top of the beach. With this in mind, they are built with long bilge keels; the only modification in their design for lake or harbour use is that the keels are shorter. It takes about six months to build one of these boats.

Beach pebbles were once used extensively in building, and particularly in cobbling. The yards of the neighbourhood were rich in patterned pebbling, plenty of which can be seen in the towns and villages, although most of the farmyards have been concreted over. They were used for walls as well, and on the beaches, particularly at Axmouth, pebble-picking was a livelihood. There was a depot nearby at Seaton and on the harbour there is still a platform where the graded pebbles were stacked. They had different names according to size, and semi-precious stones such as garnet and jasper were sold to dealers who walked the harbour wall carrying trays for their purchases.

The geological formations of the coastline, its cliffs changing sharply from red sandstone to yellow greensand, to chalk at Beer, and then to shale, has invited several types of quarrying. Red sandstone churches and houses were built from stone quarries between Beer and Salcombe Mouth in a number of small (now overgrown) workings. One has recently been reopened to repair the south tower of Exeter Cathedral, but most are now completely disused. Beer stone, mellow and honey-coloured, has been worked at least since the building of Honeyditches Roman villa on Seaton Down (now covered by a housing estate). It is to be seen in many local buildings, including the churches at Ottery St Mary, Honiton and Axminster, and Exeter Cathedral. Perhaps it is shown to its best advantage in Bovey House, Beer, a small Tudor manor house, now a hotel.

Beer Quarries are great ringing underground chambers, almost

A clinker-built boat made at Seaton

like churches themselves, and, in fact, in one of them a chapel was once carved in the living rock, perhaps for the Catholic family at Bovey House. It was removed intact in the nineteenth century and its carvings distributed to local churches. When the workings were in full use – from Roman times until the beginning of this century – waggons and horses would be driven right inside to collect the building stone. It is easy to trace the different periods of extraction by the tools used on the soft stone, which has the merit of being easy to cut and which hardens in the air to a durable material, able to take weights of many tons. Blocks of up to eight tons have been cut out of the rock. Exeter Cathedral kept detailed survey maps of the quarries to ensure a consistency in the quality of stone used for alterations and improvements over several hundred years. The graffitti of the stone cutters and the marks of their candles on the walls lead the observer to wonder about the lives of the quarrymen. Some families were represented by as many as five generations. In 1984 these quarries were opened to the public for the first time.

Other uses to which the rocks of the area have been put include a gun-flint industry on Beer Head which flourished until the early nineteenth century, a gypsum mill on Branscombe beach, powered by a water-wheel, also closed in the nineteenth century, and a malachite quarry for the copper industry, above Branscombe, long since closed. Near to the Beer stone adits are some large, commercially worked limekilns, and the remains of other older agricultural limekilns can be seen at Tidwell Mount, Ladram Bay, and on Budleigh Salterton beach.

Salt extraction is another ancient industry that was practised along this coast. The name Budleigh Salterton came from the salt-marshes at the mouth of the River Otter. The majority of salt workers once lived at Otterton, a mile inland, beyond the marshes. The Domesday survey mentions thirty-three in the eleventh century, more than in any other place in Devon. Some field names in Branscombe include the word 'cellar', which may stem from the Latin 'salaria'. The first historical reference to the town of Lyme Regis is of the salt rights being granted to Sherborne Abbey in the early Middle Ages. At Seaton there is a field called Saltplot between the church and the main car park. Salt was once a taxable commodity, and in Seaton church are several memorials to salt officers. One of them is known to have lived in Tudor Cottage, Fore Street. All round the coast of Britain salt extraction was carried on for local use by panning, until the efficiency of the German salt mines made this laborious process uneconomic in the seventeenth century. Salt was collected with sand into mounds and then evaporated out in large hoppers. Then it was heated in shallow containers until it crystallized. The fuel used in east Devon must have been wood. The flooding of the estuaries over the centuries has almost obliterated all signs of the industry, but at Seaton there are visible remains of at least twenty salt-pans.

There have been several industries connected with farming, as this is an agricultural area. The Otter Valley is particularly rich farming country, supporting more arable than is to be found in most of east Devon. This may explain why Otterton has such a large manor mill for its size of population (between 500 and 600 people, scarcely varying over the past two hundred years). The Domesday survey shows the mill with four pairs of stones, the number it still has. In the early Middle Ages, when the manor was held by Mont St Michel in Normandy, it was producing good white flour, and white loaves were being offered to the masters of fishing boats by the priors in part-payment for a good catch. The manor went into private hands at the dissolution of the monasteries, but the mill continued to flourish on the same site. In the mid-nineteenth century it had fine French millstones and was sending flour fifty miles or so away to Plymouth by coasting vessels down the Exe estuary and along the coast. There is a certain pride in the dedications of an Otterton miller on his millstones, one of which reads:

This stone worked the first time, tis true
May 1st, 1862

One of the millstones at Otterton Mill

Although the mill declined, and finally went out of production in 1959, it has been restored and now grinds wholemeal flour and has a museum, bakery and restaurant attached to it. The machinery spans three hundred years, and there are two low-breast-shot water-wheels inside the building, one of which is used for grinding and operating the sack hoist.

Along the coastal strip there are several other mills of interest. Manor Mill at Branscombe is owned by the National Trust. It is not open to visitors, but may be seen from the public footpath along the lower part of the valley. At Lyme Regis the Town Mill was mentioned in Domesday, and so was Uplyme Mill, both of which are worth looking at from the outside.

We have plenty of documentary evidence of fulling mills in the Otter valley serving the woollen mills of Ottery St Mary until the industry declined in the seventeenth century. There was one at Dotton and another at Otterton. Fulling was the process of teazing woollen cloth to give it body, rolling it and stamping it with weights, often powered by water. A Tudor bench-end in East Budleigh church (see illustration) shows a man, perhaps a fuller, with a pair of fulling shears and a bundle of teazles, which were used to raise the pile of the cloth. Soapwort, the Roman 'saponaria', one of the most ancient

Inside Otterton Mill

cleansing agents, was used to clean the cloth, and it may still be found along the Otter near the sites of the fulling mills.

To think of food in Devon is to think of clotted cream and cider and home baking. These are traditions that the tourist trade has helped to keep alive, although production tends now to be on a larger scale and in fewer farms than in the past.

Clotted cream is made by standing the milk in a wide, shallow pan over a gentle heat for a whole day without boiling, then allowing it to cool in the pan overnight and skimming off the thick cream the next morning. Signs outside farmhouses advertising cream made in this way can be seen all over the east Devon countryside, as can the notices for 'Cream teas', without which delicacy a holiday in the South-West would be unthinkable.

East Devon has lost many of its cider orchards, but they were so numerous that the countryside is still peppered with orchard trees. A lease dating from 1814 in Otterton Mill Museum directs the miller to renew apple trees as they decay, the varieties first being

Bench-end in East Budleigh church

approved by the landlord, and to manure the orchard well. An old song sung by Devon labourers includes the following verse:

> Brown bread with holes in it,
> Skim milk with eyes in it,
> Hard work and no beer,
> Hanged if I bide wi'it.
> But hard cider as much as you please,
> Loose your teeth and bow your knees,
> Sour your breath and make you wheeze,
> Turn your words to stings of bees,
> Thin your blood and kill your fleas,
> Hard cider as much as you please.

Sugar is not added to the apple juice in the fermenting of farm cider. First the apples are crushed and then the fruit is pressed in a cider press, sometimes with sacks or straw between the layers. Then the pummace is poured into large containers and allowed to ferment with its own wild yeasts. After the first violent fermentation is over, the cider is racked into barrels and kept, singing gently to itself, until its natural sugars are used up. It is drunk after about six months. (The cottage cider press in the illustration can be seen in the James Countryside Museum, Bicton Park.)

There are numerous small bakeries in east Devon, but one of the most interesting is at Branscombe, where the oven is still fired with faggots. Shavings or kindling wood are laid in the centre of the brick oven and then faggot wood is thrust inside and lit. In two hours or so the oven is heated through and the fire allowed to die down.

The bakery at Branscombe

Then the oven door is opened, the charcoal scraped out and allowed to drop through the slot at the oven door. After this the whole oven is wiped with a clean mop dipped in hot water and then it is closed for a little longer, leaving a small amount of steam inside, before it is filled with bread for baking. The beautiful crisp loaves come out an hour or so later. The long scrubbed table, the meal vats and the flagged floor in Branscombe bakery are a reminder of what small bakeries were all once like.

Two industries survive from the days of horse power in this area: the forge and the tannery. At Otterton there is a forge still in use and at Branscombe there is another, attractively thatched, belonging to the National Trust. The farrier is a woman, and she finds plenty of work shoeing riding horses as well as doing wrought-iron work. (This is not the only industry along the coast where a woman is doing work traditionally associated with men: at Otterton the miller is a woman.)

A few miles inland is Baker's Tannery at Colyton, one of the few places still using the old oak-bark method of curing leather. Hides are obtained from Ireland and the hair is removed by placing them in lime baths for three to four weeks. After that they are cured in pits with shredded oak bark for ten months, before being cleaned and rolled. The oak bark comes from the Lake District and it is shredded at the tannery by breakers operated by a water-wheel. Most of the leather is for saddlery and horse-harness, although a proportion of it goes for orthopaedic use.

The forge at Branscombe

Lacemaking at Beer in the mid-nineteenth century

Outside Beer Quarries in the mid-nineteenth century

Until recently, lacemaking was a cottage industry in east Devon, through which the women supplemented the incomes of their farming and fishing husbands. East Devon lace is a pillow-lace, mainly worked by making sprigs which are then appliquéd to a net background. In the past, guipère lace was also made; in this, each part of the design is joined by 'brides', large loose net-work, part of the lace itself. The traditional motifs found in Devon lace (or, as it is often called, Honiton lace, as the town was once the focal point for the industry) include birds, butterflies and recognizable varieties of flowers. Children used once to learn the industry at the village lace schools, some of which can still be seen, as can the lace shops where

lacemakers exchanged their sprigs for groceries as recently as eighty years ago. During the eighteenth century there were twenty lace schools in Exmouth, but following a disastrous slump, aggravated by the introduction of machine-made net, none was left in 1887.

Devon lace was made for four hundred years in great quantities until changing fashions and the costs of such labour-intensive work in this century killed the industry, so that it is now done just as a hobby. Some of the best lace was made at Branscombe where the Tucker workshop employed 500 workers at its peak. Fine work was produced at Beer as well, where Queen Victoria's wedding dress was made. This was a great achievement, involving the whole female community over a period of many months and ending in the nervous collapse of Jane Bidney, the organizer. The royal family have been patrons of the Devon lacemakers since Queen Charlotte had a Honiton-lace wedding dress made in 1760.

East Devon is by no means an industrial area, in that few, if any, of the traditional industries mentioned here have built up to provide work for more people or to increase the variety of goods available. However, the skills which have gone into the exploitation of the natural resources in this small stretch of Devon are a reminder that the inhabitants have always tried by instinct to make the best possible use of what is around them. There is great pleasure in discovering the simple and effective ways this has been done in the past.

Industries still operating

Fishermen operate fishing trips in the summer months from Ladram Bay, Branscombe, Beer, Seaton and Lyme Regis. They can be seen at work in all the coastal towns.

Mears of Seaton   Makers of clinker-built boats.

Beer Quarry   Commercial limekilns.

Otterton Mill   Wholemeal flour production. Bakery and restaurant selling own baked goods. Baking daily.

Branscombe Bakery   Bread baked daily.

Numerous farms make and sell clotted cream. A few make farm cider.

Otterton forge   Shoeing and wrought-iron work.

Branscombe Forge   Shoeing and wrought-iron work.

Baker's Tannery, Colyton   Oak-bark tanning. Shop for leather goods. Tannery open on Wednesday mornings to visitors.

Museums illustrating traditional industries

Beer Quarries   Open to the public daily, Easter – September.

Otterton Mill Museum   Open throughout the year, 10.30 – 5.30 daily, 2 – 5 winter week-ends.

The James Countryside Museum   Open Easter – September. Inside Bicton Park.

East Devon lace may be seen at the following museums on or near the coast: Fairlynch Museum, Budleigh Salterton; Otterton Mill Museum; Sidmouth Museum; Allhallows Museum, Honiton.

11 | AGRICULTURE

Farming is the largest industry in south-west England, having a larger turnover than any other industry and employing an extensive area of land. Even now farmers grow the greater part of the food we eat, and if a national emergency were to strike the nation, nearly all the food we would need could be provided by home production.

On the east Devon coast most of the land is farmed by family farming businesses which derive their entire livelihood from the crops and livestock they produce. Behind the farmers, and very much part of the farming community, lies a vast array of supporting industries and professionals who are vital to agriculture.

Farming is a modern and highly technical industry, but conservation is important to the farmer to maintain the natural beauty of the countryside and the ecological balance. Farmers must use cultivation techniques which lead to a stable soil structure, minimum loss of moisture and a high level of humus in the soil to maintain or improve its fertility.

The farms mould well into the beautiful landscape of this coastal stretch. In some places their fields reach right to the cliff edge, while in others the farms stand back behind trees and woodland, but all provide colour and variety as the farming seasons progress through the year.

In most places the fields are divided by hedges or by hedge-banks, which are a particular feature of Devon. If these are well maintained they provide an excellent stockproof boundary, better than the field fences found in many parts of England. They are also a haven for wildlife, providing shelter from wind and storm. Most of the hedges are cut annually, outside the bird-nesting season, using tractor-mounted flail mowers, giving the now-characteristic smooth and neat finish.

Harvesting potatoes at South Farm near Budleigh Salterton

Crops

Corn

Wheat and barley are grown in profusion in this area. The crops are now generally sown into a fine and carefully prepared seedbed during September, October and November so that the plants grow slowly and develop their roots during the winter in readiness for the main growing seasons of spring and summer. Notice the wheel marks through the crops made by the farmer on his tractor when he was either feeding the crop with fertilizer or tending to its health by spray treatment. These are necessary to sustain the crops during their long growing season. As the seasons progress the crops grow tall and turn from a lush green to a rich golden brown, adding to the interest and colour of the landscape.

In late July and throughout August and September combine harvesters can be seen moving steadily through the ripened crops, starting with the barley and then going on to the wheat. These vastly complex machines cut and lift the crops from the fields, thrash out the grain and blow away the chaff, leaving behind the straw ready to be baled up for use as livestock bedding or fodder.

Some of the larger farms have their own drying and storage facilities for the grain; others send theirs to large installations at such places as Exmouth, Exeter and Cullompton. Throughout the year the dried grain is transported from the stores to its various markets in accordance with demand and here co-operation between farmers, hauliers and millers is essential.

Wheat is used mainly for human consumption in such things as bread and biscuits. Some is exported to Europe, the Mediterranean and the Middle East through the small dock at Exmouth. The best barley is used for malting, while the remainder is made into feed for

Open agricultural landscape on the cliffs west of Sidmouth

cattle, sheep, pigs, poultry and horses, helping to feed the large numbers of farm animals in the South West.

Oilseed rape

A newcomer to the agricultural scene in this area is oilseed rape, which adds a bright splash of colour. Rape is sown in September and grows rapidly into a lush green crop, tall in the spring and producing a dramatic bright yellow flower in May which later fades to a dark golden colour as the plants run to seed. The crop is harvested in August. Combine harvesters thrash out the tiny black seeds, which are dried and transported to specialized crushing plants where the oil is extracted to be used as cooking oil.

Rape is a welcome crop as, apart from its striking appearance, it provides a break between corn crops in the farming rotation, thus improving the fertility of the land.

Vegetable and root crops

The sharp-eyed traveller will notice some fields, particularly in the area between Sidmouth and Budleigh Salterton, of potatoes, cabbages, cauliflowers, carrots and other vegetables and root crops. The mild climate of the south-west and in particular the relatively frost-free conditions found close to the sea are particularly suitable for growing vegetables.

These crops add further interest and variety to the coastal scene and provide activity all the year round as they are harvested daily for shops selling fresh vegetables. These are labour-intensive crops, involving many people in planting, harvesting and packing.

Grass

Many fields along the coast are not suitable for regular ploughing and cultivation because they are too steep or stony. Here grass grows in abundance and is an important crop providing fodder for the livestock on the many farms. The grass has to be grown well and looked after carefully as it is used to provide both direct grazing and a supply of fodder for the long winter months.

Grass which is harvested is now generally made into silage. It is cut and later lifted, chopped and blown into large trailers by forage harvesters, a common sight on the coast in May and June in particular. The cut grass is put into silage pits at the many farmsteads, where it is rolled to expel the air and then covered to make a succulent feed for cattle and sheep.

In the summer some grass is cut and dried on the ground to make hay. It is then packed into bales to be carted to the farmsteads and stored under cover. Bales of hay are simple to transport and feed to animals during the winter.

Cattle

The familiar black-and-white British Fresian cows will be seen grazing in many grass fields along the east Devon coast. These cows have been bred for milk production and every year each cow produces between 1100 and 1500 gallons of milk and generally one calf.

Every day in the very early morning and again during the afternoon the keen observer will see the cows walking into the various farmsteads to be milked in large and highly mechanized milking-parlours. The milk is stored in refrigerated tanks and collected once a day in large road tankers, which take it inland to one of the many creameries for processing. More than half the milk arrives on the doorstep as fresh milk within twenty-four hours and the rest is made into other milk-based products, such as butter, cheese, cream, chocolate, milk power and yoghourt.

About half the calves that are born are bull calves; they will be grown on and fattened to produce beef any time from one to two years after birth. The best of the heifer calves are selected and reared to join the dairy herd when they are two years old and have had their first calf.

Most of the other cattle on the farms have been bred to produce high quality Devon beef and when they are fully grown they will be transported to one of the abattoirs in inland towns, possibly at Torrington or Exeter. Much of the beef produced on Devon farms is exported out of the region to other parts of Britain or overseas to Europe and other more distant markets.

The regular traveller will notice that in the winter hardly any cattle are to be seen in the fields in this area. At that time the grass must rest so the cattle live in specialized housing and are fed on hay or silage and barley-based concentrate feed.

Sheep

Sheep will be found grazing the poorer pastures along the coast. There are many different breeds of sheep and the selection of a particular breed is very much a matter of the personal choice of each individual farmer.

About half the ewes produce twin lambs each year and the others single lambs or triplets. The lambs are born at any time between November and May, depending on the breed of sheep and the policy of the farmer. It is natural for the ewes to have their lambs outside, however, the trees, hedge-banks and the natural undulations in the landscape provide plenty of shelter and ewes which are about to produce their lambs may sometimes be seen selecting a suitably sheltered place in the field.

The young lambs grow fast. They have a short life and only three to five months after birth the majority have left the farms and have

The coast path following field boundaries near Ladram Bay

passed through one of the inland abattoirs on their way to the dinner table in this country or abroad. The lambs which remain grow up and join the ewe flock and have lambs of their own one year after birth.

The ewes change their appearance once a year when they are shorn. The fleece is sold to be spun into wool to make knitwear, tweeds and carpets.

Trees

The whole of the Heritage Coast is marked by the profusion and variety of the trees. From the individual tree standing sentinel on the edge of a field, to the rows of trees between fields or marking the many valleys, their importance as part of the landscape is obvious. To the farmer they are important because they provide shelter for his animals in times of storm. To the observer the changing colours of oak, birch, maple, larch and many others are a constant source of joy.

Parts of the coast were seriously denuded of trees in the 1970s when Dutch elm disease took its toll as it swept through the area. Some dead elms remain but most have gone.

The quiet industrial revolution that has taken place in farming since the 1930s has brought many changes to the Heritage Coast. In practical terms fields have become bigger, ground preparation and harvesting are carried out faster and the amount of food which the land now produces has been multiplied many times. In human terms the change has been immense. The huge number of people who once worked on the land has now shrunk to a few highly skilled people operating very complex machinery backed by continual scientific improvements.

This has changed the nature of the villages and hamlets. Places such as Otterton, Salcombe Regis, Branscombe and Beer, which were once largely populated by people who worked on the farms or in the woodlands or provided a direct service to the farms, are now inhabited mainly by people who have no direct agricultural connections. The villages and hamlets themselves have been developed and expanded to provide for the needs of those working in towns but wishing to live in the country, as well as the retired and the tourists.

Thus the town has come to the country and, by the same token, the country has gone to the town because the services required by the farmer – be it the haulier, the machinery supplier and repairer, the veterinary surgeon, the miller or the builder – are now to be found in such places as Exeter, Exmouth, Sidmouth and Honiton.

The East Devon Heritage Coast remains a place of quiet industry and beauty. It is a place for the farmer to work with care and for the visitor and walker to cherish.

BIBLIOGRAPHY

Chapter 2
Durrance, E. M. and Laming, D. J. C. (eds) *The Geology of Devon* (*University of Exeter*, 1982)
Institute of Geological Sciences *British Regional Geology: South West England* Fourth edition 1975 (H.M.S.O.)
Perkins, J. W. *Geology explained in South and East Devon* (David & Charles, 1971)

Chapter 3
Atlas of the Devon Flora (Devonshire Association, 1984)
Coastlines of Devon (Devon County Council, 1980)
Hepburn, Ian *Flowers of the Coast* (Collins, 1962)
Rose, Francis *The Wild Flower Key* (Warne, 1981)

Chapter 4
Davies, S. *The Birds of the West Country* (Royal Society for the Protection of Birds, 1980)
Holden, P. and Sharrock, J. T. R. *RSPB Book of British Birds* (Macmillan, 1984)
Moore, R. *The Birds of Devon* (David & Charles, 1969)
Norman, D. and Tucker, V. *Where to Watch Birds in Devon and Cornwall* (Croom Helm, 1984)
Peterson, Mountfort and Hollom *A Field Guide to the Birds of Britain and Europe* (Collins, revised edition 1974)

Chapter 5
Campbell, A. C. and Nicholls, James *Hamlyn Guide to the Seashore and Shallow Seas of Britain and Europe* (Hamlyn, 1976)
Devon Trust for Nature Conservation *Exploring the Seashore*

Chapter 6
The archaeological background is most readily found in Aileen Fox's *South-West England* (David & Charles, 1973), whilst Professor W. G. Hoskins' *Devon* (David & Charles, 1972) gives extensive historical information. The same author's *Fieldwork in Local History* (Faber, second edition 1982) is also full of interest.
Two recent Devon County Council publications – *Devon's Traditional Buildings* (1978) and *Archaeology of the Devon Landscape* (1981) – are now out of print but may be obtained from local libraries. Both contain essays on different subjects relevant to East Devon. Recent works of local interest are Ursula Brighouse's *Woodbury – the View from the Beacon* (Woodbury News, 1981) and Catherine Linehan's *Peter Orlando Hutchinson of Sidmouth Devon* (published by the author, 1983). Useful guide books to several of the parish churches are also available.

Booklets and articles relating to East Devon sites are available from the Devon Archaeological Society. Details of membership, etc., can be obtained from the Society, c/o Royal Albert Memorial Museum, Queen Street, Exeter. Inquiries about specific sites should be addressed to the Sites and Monuments Register, Devon County Council, County Hall, Exeter.

Chapter 7
The Annual Reports on Devon Folklore contained within Vols 1–116 of the *Transactions of the Devonshire Association* (1864-1984)
Devon and Cornwall Notes and Queries
The Devon Folklife Register (housed at Rougemont House Museum, Exeter)
Coxhead, J. R. W. *Smuggling Days in Devon* (Raleigh Press, 1956)
Delderfield, E. R. *The Raleigh Country* (Raleigh Press, 1949)
Whitlock, Ralph *The Folklore of Devon* (Batsford, 1977)

Chapter 8
Delderfield, E. R. *Exmouth Milestones* (Raleigh Press, 1948)
Everett, W. *Memorials of Exmouth* (Second edition 1885)
Farr, G. *Wreck and Rescue on the South Coast of Devon* (Chapter 10)
Illustrated Guide to Branscombe (c. 1900)
Larn, R. *Devon Shipwrecks* (Chapter 5) (David & Charles, 1974)
Oppenheim, M. *Maritime History of Devon* (University of Exeter, 1968)
The Lower Otter Valley. Sketches on Local History (Otter Valley Association, 1984)
Rattenbury, Jack *Memoirs of a smuggler* (Frank Graham, 1964)
Sir John Eliot and the Vice-Admiralty of Devon (Camden Miscellany, Volume 17, 1940)
Teignmouth, Lord and Harper, C. G. *The Smugglers* (1923)

Chapter 9
Brunskill, R. W. *Illustrated Handbook of Vernacular Architecture* (Faber, second edition 1978)
Hunt, P. J. *Devon's Age of Elegance* (Devon Books, 1984)
Devon's Traditional Buildings (Devon County Council, 1978)
Hoskins, W. G. *Devon* (David & Charles, 1972)
Hoskins, W. G. *Old Devon* (David & Charles, 1966)

Chapter 10
Devon's Traditional Buildings (Devon County Council, 1978)
Greenhow, D. *Devon Mill* (C. Skilton, 1979)
Hoskins, W. G. *Devon* (David & Charles, 1972)
Minchinton, W. *Devon at Work* (David & Charles, 1974)
Tomlinson, M. *Three Generations in the Honiton Lace Trade* (1983)

INDEX OF PLACES

Follow the Country Code

Enjoy the countryside and respect its life
and work
Guard against all risk of fire
Fasten all gates
Keep your dogs under close control
Keep to public paths across farmland
Use gates and stiles to cross fences,
hedges and walls
Leave livestock, crops and machinery
alone
Take your litter home
Help to keep all water clean
Protect wildlife, plants and trees
Take special care on country roads
Make no unnecessary noise

There is now an Access Charter, prepared by the Countryside
Commission, which gives information about the public's rights of
access in the countryside.